GREATER
EXPECTATIONS

A New Vision for Learning as a Nation Goes to College

NATIONAL PANEL REPORT

Association
of American
Colleges and
Universities

Published by the

ASSOCIATION OF AMERICAN COLLEGES AND UNIVERSITIES

1818 R Street, NW, Washington, DC 20009-1604

www.aacu.org

Copyright © 2002

ISBN 0-911696-92-x

This text is available in its entirety at www.greaterexpectations.org

To order print copies of this publication or to find out about other AAC&U
publications, e-mail pub_desk@aacu.org or call 202/387-3760.

*Published with support of The Pew Charitable Trusts. The opinions expressed in this
report are those of the authors and do not necessarily reflect the views of The Pew
Charitable Trusts.*

Greater Expectations National Panel

Contents

ACKNOWLEDGMENTS

THIS REPORT REPRESENTS the sustained and collective work of many individuals. Over a period of two years, the twenty-five *Greater Expectations National Panel* members learned about the issues and taught one another. Judith Ramaley, as chair, skillfully guided expansive conversations. Faculty and administrators from the *Greater Expectations Consortium on Quality Education* met with the panelists to describe their experiences and, by so doing, helped shape the New Academy herein described. Carol Schneider, president of the Association of American Colleges and Universities (AAC&U), conceived of Greater Expectations more than three years ago. Her insight and foresight were the generative sparks for the panel's analysis. AAC&U staff members —most notably Deborah Yarrow and Ross Miller—made certain the panel meetings were perfectly run and well recorded. The latter, as the project's researcher and archivist, kept everyone well informed and up-to-date. Other AAC&U contributors included Debra Humphreys, Cathleen Fleck, Sally Clarke, Alma Clayton-Pedersen, Julie Warren, Bridget Puzon, Noreen O'Connor, Maryrose Flanigan, Robert Shoenberg, Barbara Hill, Irena Makarushka, and Edgar Beckham. Truly this was a collaborative effort. Representatives from regional and specialized accrediting associations, participating in the Greater Expectations Project on Accreditation and Assessment led by John Nichols, refined the panel's understanding of important outcomes for college learning. Robert Kenny contributed to the writing, Katherine Oliver to the discussions, Clifford Adelman to the briefings. The Greater Expectations work would not have been possible without the support of The Pew Charitable Trusts, Carnegie Corporation of New York, and the Fund for the Improvement of Postsecondary Education. All three funders participated in the National Panel's deliberations and brought invaluable insights to the meetings. Particular thanks go to Russell Edgerton, Ellen Wert, Donald Stewart, Daniel Fallon, and Neil Grabois. Finally, thousands of readers around the country took the not-inconsiderable time to read drafts of the report as it unfolded and to provide their comments. The report is finer because of their dedication.

ANDREA LESKES
Vice President for Education and Quality Initiatives, AAC&U
Director, Greater Expectations

PREFACE

THROUGHOUT ITS HISTORY, the United States has asked much of higher education: to prepare leaders, train employees, provide the creative base for scientific and artistic discovery, transmit past culture, create new knowledge, redress the legacies of discrimination, and ensure continuation of democratic principles. The balance among these needs has shifted over time in response to many factors and will undoubtedly continue to do so.

As we enter a new millennium, we find ourselves in a turbulent time, having almost completed transformation from an industrial to a knowledge-based society. Changing times require alert self-reflection and creativity. What should be higher education's role today and for the near future? What are the central aims and essential practices of college study?

College education benefits individuals but also importantly benefits our entire nation. Unlike the single, unified system found in many other countries, we have a vibrant enterprise of private and state-supported colleges and universities. Institutions with diverse missions have flourished, from community colleges to research universities; small, rural residential colleges to large, urban comprehensive universities; church-affiliated campuses to minority-serving institutions, and everything in between. Our network of higher education spans the nation, forming a rich resource of multiple approaches for multiple audiences as the United States, more than any other country, moves toward universal participation.

Engendering self-reflection among such dispersed and varied institutions presents a particular challenge. The Association of American Colleges and Universities assumed the facilitator's role in 2000 with its initiative *Greater Expectations: The Commitment to Quality as a Nation Goes to College.*

At the center of Greater Expectations is an analysis of the challenges facing higher education and an honest appraisal of our successes and failures in meeting them. A broadly constituted National Panel was appointed to this task. The panel was charged with informing itself thoroughly and listening to many voices in conducting the analysis.

The panel's deliberations, summarized in this report, have led to a recommendation to rethink what we should expect from, and how we should provide, college education in the twenty-first century. The report challenges all stakeholders to unite for collective action, creating a coherent educational system designed to help all students achieve the greater expectations that are the hallmark of our time.

In its work, the panel modeled this collaborative action and the commitment to continuous learning that is a central outcome of college study. The conversations—rich and complex in the extreme—deepened the understanding of every panel member who came to see both the limitations of her or his original perspective and its contribution to a fuller picture.

Our report is organized for diverse uses and employs multiple forms of communication. Throughout the written document, stories provide examples of exciting innovations, while action steps suggest what to do next. A Web site (www.greaterexpectations.org), allied with the report, permits individuals or stakeholder groups to read or "drill down" through the text in various ways. Some may follow links to research supporting the analysis, others may seek out additional models of promising curricular practice, and still others may choose to share the executive overview with friends and colleagues.

The panel's work focuses on college-level learning in accredited institutions and on student preparation for such learning. Although the analysis is relatively complete, the complexity of the issues prevented close examination of them all. So while the financing of higher educa-tion, for example, is intimately related to quality, a thorough posing and answering of questions about funding is beyond the scope of this report.

The panel took seriously the charge of depicting problems and outlining solutions. And so it offers the vision of a New Academy built on the experiences of those very practitioners—at the collegiate and also at the secondary school level—who have begun changing what and how college students learn. Formally advising the panel were twenty-two campuses from around the country, selected for the power and scope of their improvements in undergraduate learning. This Consortium on Quality Education, part of the Greater Expectations Initiative, met repeatedly with the panel and shared new approaches to defining the purposes of an undergraduate education and to promoting learning. (See page 60 for a list of Consortium campuses.) To them and others who have served as leaders of the present and inspirations for the future, the panel expresses its deep admiration. ■

For the Greater Expectations National Panel,

Judith Ramaley
Assistant Director for Education and Human Resources, National Science Foundation
Panel Chair

Andrea Leskes
Vice President for Education and Quality Initiatives, AAC&U
Director, Greater Expectations, Panel Member, *ex-officio*

EXECUTIVE OVERVIEW

THE UNITED STATES IS FAST APPROACHING UNIVERSAL PARTICIPATION IN HIGHER EDUCATION. Recognizing the transformative importance of this development, the Association of American Colleges and Universities launched *Greater Expectations: The Commitment to Quality as a Nation Goes to College*. As part of that initiative, a national panel of top education, private sector, public policy, and community leaders spent the past two years analyzing higher education in the United States today. The report, *Greater Expectations: A New Vision for Learning as a Nation Goes to College*, details their findings and recommendations.

The report calls for a dramatic reorganization of undergraduate education to ensure that all college aspirants receive not just access to college, but an education of lasting value. The panel offers a new vision that will promote the kind of learning students need to meet emerging challenges in the workplace, in a diverse democracy, and in an interconnected world. The report also proposes a series of specific actions and collaborations to raise substantially the quality of student learning in college.

The panel concludes that change is urgently needed. Even as college attendance is rising, the performance of too many students is faltering. Public policies have focused on getting students into college, but not on what they are expected to accomplish once there. The result is that the college experience is a revolving door for millions of students, while the college years are poorly spent by many others.

Broad, meaningful reform in higher education is long overdue. The near-universal demand for higher learning in the United States creates new urgency, opportunity, and responsibility to revitalize the practice of undergraduate education.

Some colleges and universities already are making the kinds of learning-centered changes the report recommends. The panel studied pace-setting reforms on campuses across the country, and worked in partnership with a set of competitively selected

"Greater Expectations" colleges, community colleges, and universities representing both private and public education.

These campus examples of Greater Expectations in action give reason for hope that Americans can, and will, create a new national commitment to educational excellence for every college student.

College in the Twenty-First Century

College attendance has grown so rapidly over the past four decades that now 75 percent of high school graduates get some postsecondary education within two years of receiving their diplomas. Older adults, also, have enrolled in increasing numbers. A college degree has in many ways become what a high school diploma became 100 years ago—the path to a successful career and to knowledgeable citizenship.

Students are flocking to college because the world is complex, turbulent, and more reliant on knowledge than ever before. But educational practices invented when higher education served only the few are increasingly disconnected from the needs of contemporary students.

Today's college students come from an extraordinarily diverse array of national, racial/ethnic, and socio-economic backgrounds. They bring great vitality to campus, but also place significant new demands on faculty knowledge and skill.

Students also attend college today in very different ways. A rapidly rising majority pursues the degree by attending two or more institutions. Part-time enrollment and distance learning are now common. Many students navigate this new terrain without clear direction or educational maps, collecting credits haphazardly as they go.

Preparation for higher learning has not kept pace with access. Less than one-half of students who enter college directly from high school complete even a minimally defined college preparatory program. Only 40 percent of school teachers hold the high expectations for performance that would ready students for college-level work. Once in college, 53 percent of all students must take remedial courses. Those students requiring the most remedial work are the least likely to persist and graduate.

These far-reaching developments call for new approaches to educational quality. But needed reforms are hindered by the absence of broadly shared agreement about what students ought to accomplish in college.

Many students and parents see college primarily as the springboard to employment; they want job-related courses. Policy makers view college as a spur to regional economic growth, and they urge highly targeted workforce development. Business leaders seek graduates who can think analytically, communicate effectively, and solve problems in collaboration with diverse colleagues, clients, or customers. Faculty members want students to develop sophisticated intellectual skills and also to learn about science, society, the arts, and human culture. For the higher education community as a whole, college is a time when faculty and students can explore important issues in ways that respect a variety of viewpoints and deepen understanding.

A meaningful commitment to educational excellence begins with agreement about the most important goals for student learning. The National Panel report offers a contemporary and comprehensive vision for college learning —a vision that addresses the *multiple* hopes Americans hold for college education. Moreover, this vision engages the role that higher learning plays in creating a just democracy, cooperation among diverse peoples, and a sustainable world.

Barriers to Quality from School to College

The United States can take great pride in the progress it has made in giving more students access to college. But even this work remains both unfinished and insufficient. It is unfinished because access continues to be inequitable, especially for the poor and most minority groups. It is insufficient because many students do not succeed once in college and fail to gain the kind of powerful learning that equips them for a world in flux. Formidable barriers to excellence stand in their way.

Despite years of efforts to improve, secondary education in many school districts continues to be seriously deficient, resulting in students who are underprepared for college-level work. State-mandated tests—the center-piece of the school reform agenda—often reflect a limited interpretation of learning, overemphasizing memorization of discrete facts at the expense of deeper understanding and its application. Faced with many pressures, including high stakes testing and financial constraints, schools place too little emphasis on the analytical, integrative, and practical skills graduates need.

There is also a disturbing misalignment between high school exit require-ments and college entry expectations. Few colleges regularly share with secondary schools what incoming first year students should know and be able to do. "College" courses in high school (as well as remedial courses in college) have proliferated, despite the absence of guiding principles about what characterizes college-level learning. Many colleges and universities have begun to encourage more in-depth, investigative, or research-based learning even in the first year, but high school and many advanced placement courses continue to feature broad surveys and superficial "coverage." The senior year of high school, which ideally should emphasize the intellectual skills expected in college, is wasted for many students.

Once enrolled in college, students face other barriers to excellence. The fragmentation of the curriculum into a collection of independently "owned" courses is itself an impediment to student accomplishment, because the different courses students take, even on the same campus, are not expected to engage or build on one another. Few maps exist to help students plan or integrate their learning as they move in and out of separately organized courses, programs, and campuses. In the absence of shared learning goals and clear expectations, a college degree more frequently certifies completion of disconnected fragments than of a coherent plan for student accomplishment.

Other barriers to quality include professors trained and rewarded more for research than for teaching, a prestige hierarchy built on reputation and resources rather than on educational success, and a lack of meaningful or comparable measurements to assess student-learning outcomes.

Many college students now juggle multiple demands, including an increased financial burden, full- or part-time employment, and family obligations. College students typically spend less than half the time on their studies that faculty expect. All these conditions complicate efforts to achieve greater expectations for aspiring college graduates— especially if these new realities are not taken into account in a comprehensive reform of undergraduate education.

The Learning Students Need for the Twenty-First Century

These barriers to quality notwithstanding, there is hope on the horizon. College faculties across the country are beginning to adopt new practices that raise the level of student effort and achievement. The Greater Expectations National Panel report and its attendant Web site (www.greaterexpectations.org) highlight many such promising innovations.

The key to successful reform is a clear focus on the kinds of learning that students need for a complex world. The panel urges an invigorated and practical liberal education as the most empowering form of learning for the twenty-first century. It makes strong recommendations about the knowledge and capacities all students should acquire—regardless of backgrounds, fields, or chosen higher education institutions.

The report further recommends that these goals for students' liberal education become the shared concern of both school *and* college. The transition from high school to college should be considered a joint responsibility of schools and higher education; it should be carefully planned. The learning outcomes needed in this new era can only be achieved when all parts of the educational experience address them.

Students will continue to pursue different specializations in college. But across all fields, the panel calls for higher education to help college students become INTENTIONAL LEARNERS who can adapt to new environments, integrate knowledge from different sources, and continue learning throughout their lives. To thrive in a complex world, these intentional learners should also become:

> EMPOWERED through the mastery of intellectual and practical skills
> INFORMED by knowledge about the natural and social worlds and about forms of inquiry basic to these studies
> RESPONSIBLE for their personal actions and for civic values.

The empowered learner. The intellectual and practical skills that students need are extensive, sophisticated, and expanding with the explosion of new technologies. As they progress through grades K-12 and the undergraduate years, and at successively more challenging levels, students should learn to:

- effectively communicate orally, visually, in writing, and in a second language
- understand and employ quantitative and qualitative analysis to solve problems
- interpret and evaluate information from a variety of sources
- understand and work within complex systems and with diverse groups
- demonstrate intellectual agility and the ability to manage change
- transform information into knowledge and knowledge into judgment and action.

The informed learner. While intellectual and practical skills are essential, so is a deeper understanding of the world students inherit, as human beings and as contributing citizens. This knowledge extends beyond core concepts to include ways of investigating human society and the natural world. Both in school and college, students should have sustained opportunities to learn about:

- the human imagination, expression, and the products of many cultures
- the interrelations within and among global and cross-cultural communities
- means of modeling the natural, social, and technical worlds
- the values and histories underlying U.S. democracy.

The responsible learner. The integrity of a democratic society depends on citizens' sense of social responsibility and ethical judgment. To develop these qualities, education should foster:

- intellectual honesty
- responsibility for society's moral health and for social justice
- active participation as a citizen of a diverse democracy
- discernment of the ethical consequences of decisions and actions
- deep understanding of one's self and respect for the complex identities of others, their histories, and their cultures.

Taken together, these outcomes form the core of a twenty-first century liberal education—liberal not in any political sense, but in terms of liberating and opening the mind, and of preparing students for responsible action. The panel calls for a new national commitment to provide an excellent liberal education to all students, not just those attending elite institutions and not just those studying traditional arts and sciences disciplines. Professional studies—such as business, education, health sciences, technologies—should also be approached as liberal education.

In this spirit, the report urges an end to the traditional, artificial distinctions between liberal and practical education. Liberal education in all fields will have the strongest impact when studies look beyond the classroom to the world's major questions, asking students to apply their developing analytical skills and ethical judgment to significant problems in the world around them. By valuing cooperative as well as individual performance, diversity as a resource for learning, real solutions to unscripted problems, and creativity as well as critical thinking, this newly pragmatic liberal education will both prepare students for a dynamic economy and build civic capacity at home and abroad.

Principles of Good Practice in the New Academy

The Greater Expectations National Panel is optimistic about the future. Liberal education has historically adapted to the needs of a changing world, and innovative approaches can already be found on every kind of campus. The next step is to create from these isolated innovations a comprehensive movement for change across the higher education landscape. The report describes a learning-centered New Academy arising from such a movement.

In this New Academy, colleges and universities will model the purposeful action—the intentionality—they expect of their students. Faculty members will focus more centrally on goals for student learning in both courses and programs, not just on the subject matter taught or the number of credits earned. Leaders will use resources strategically to build a culture centered on learning. Within a broad array of distinctive institutional missions and roles, this learning-centered New Academy will exhibit a rich and desirable diversity of approaches to education. But there will also be a shared commitment to high standards, and new collaborations that create more purposeful educational environments allowing easier passage from one educational institution to another.

Reaching ambitious goals for learning requires integrating elements of the curriculum traditionally treated as separate—general education, the major, and electives—into a coherent program. This does not mean that students will take a common set of courses. But it will require new forms of advising and alignment, both in high school and college, to help each student create a plan of study leading to the essential outcomes of a twenty-first century education. There will be many alternative paths up the educational mountain. But every student needs a sense of direction, markers as well as knowledgeable guides, and navigational tools to support the journey.

Meeting these expectations for quality will focus new attention on the culminating year of college. Both institutions and departments should set standards for achievement of skills, knowledge, and responsibility, and require advanced work that demonstrates the expected outcomes. These culminating performances, which will vary with different fields of study, ought to provide evidence that students can integrate the many parts of their education. They can show how well students actually possess the intellectual, practical, and evaluative judgment and the sense of responsibility a college degree should represent.

Higher education will need to provide both existing and future faculty and school teachers with the necessary preparation to teach effectively in new, challenging environments. The academy must also offer incentives, professional development, support, and rewards for good teaching. Finally, at both the higher and secondary education levels, the nation must develop more sophisticated, nuanced ways of assessing student learning. To build such a culture of evidence, students and faculty need tools to assess all levels of learning and to mark student progress in achieving the goals of a twenty-first century education.

Achieving Greater Expectations: A Shared Responsibility

Achieving this vision will require concerted action among all stakeholders. Learning-centered reform cannot be accomplished by any one institution or even by the higher education sector alone. Collaboration with secondary school leaders will help ensure better preparation of all high school students for rigorous college learning. Collaboration among policy makers at the state and federal levels will focus public policy and resources on the quality of students' liberal education. Cooperation with accrediting agencies will further reinforce the national commitment to connect evidence of student accomplishment with judgments about educational quality.

The report of the Greater Expectations National Panel also presents a preliminary set of recommendations that engages many groups, including those in secondary and higher education, as well as policy makers, business leaders, boards of trustees, school boards, the media, college students, and their parents.

The Greater Expectations National Panel urges all citizens to take part in creating a society where learning is prized and everyone has access to an excellent education. Ultimately, the nation's future and its place in the world depend on a new vision for learning as the nation goes to college. ■

CHAPTER I

COLLEGE IN THE 21ST CENTURY

The century is dawning ...

IN HIGHER EDUCATION AS CHARLES DICKENS'S BEST OF TIMES/WORST OF TIMES. Optimists see more Americans than ever before attending college. Critics, on the other hand, note that many never finish their college studies, or graduate only to find themselves underprepared for professional, personal, and community life in a rapidly changing world.

As increasing numbers of people seek collegiate education, the country needs to ensure them not simply access to college, but an education of real and lasting value. The unprecedented expansion of college enrollments creates an extraordinary opportunity to prepare the informed citizens and competent employees needed for the new knowledge-based society. Yet there is a very real danger that the United States will squander this opportunity, although the consequences of failure are severe. Each individual dropped by the wayside represents a loss—personal, economic, social, and intellectual. When many are dropped, the nation itself is impoverished. Universal readiness for and success in obtaining a college education of high quality are democratic values, moral imperatives, and economic necessities. The country deserves no less.

We are a college-going nation ...

IN A NEW AND EXCITING WAY. College attendance in the United States has grown so rapidly over the past four decades that now 75 percent of high school graduates get some postsecondary education within two years of receiving their diplomas. Student aspirations are even loftier, with nearly 90 percent saying they hope to attend college.[1] Older adults, too, have recognized the benefits of college study and account for more than one-third of matriculants.[2] Possession of a college degree today means substantially

The Nation Goes to College

Access has increased:
- 75 percent of high school graduates continue their studies[4]
- 90 percent of high school seniors expect to attend college[5]
- minorities now comprise 28 percent of college students, although some groups remain underrepresented[6]
- 57 percent of 2000 graduates were women; in 1961 over 60% were men[7]
- growing numbers of students are over age twenty-five.

Preparation still lags:
- only 47 percent of high school graduates complete college prep curricula[8]
- 40 percent of students in four-year colleges and 53 percent overall take remedial courses[9]
- the more remedial study students need, the lower their prospects of graduating.[10]

Attendance patterns have changed:
- 58 percent of bachelor's degree recipients attend two or more colleges[11]
- 28 percent of undergraduate students attend part-time[12]
- 73 percent of all undergraduates are non-traditional students.[13]

Enrollment will continue to grow, as the student body becomes more diverse:
- by 2015, 1 to 2 million additional young adults will seek access to college, many from low-income and minority families[14]
- while most growth is expected in the traditional age bracket, students over age twenty-five are also projected to increase: 14 percent by 2010.[15]

what a high school diploma meant a hundred years ago; it is the passport to most careers, and without it, people can find themselves trapped in unrewarding jobs.

As college attendance rates have risen, so too has the diversity of the student body. Teaching techniques, course content, and college organization that may have been adequate when mostly white and privileged young men went to college, now need to be diversified as well. With college serving a much larger part of society, strong pressure exists to make education truly effective. Available research on teaching has the potential to improve every student's achievement, but has yet to influence significantly either schools or colleges.

Attendance patterns have changed as well. Forty years ago, the typical student entered a college at age eighteen and emerged from it four years later as a graduate. Although significant groups of students still follow this pattern, it is no longer the norm. Many undergraduates are older, resuming interrupted studies or attending part-time as they work and raise families. In their progression toward a degree, large numbers of students enroll at two, three, or more institutions, also taking courses online. For them college can be a revolving door. In the past, students relied on one institution to provide degree programs and, they hoped, to deliver a logically sequenced education. While coherence may have been illusory even then, newer attendance patterns place greater responsibility on students themselves to create meaningful learning from a supermarket of choices. If not well advised about how to plan an education, students can waste time and money—and jeopardize their futures—even as society is deprived of a well-educated citizenry.

At the same time that colleges admit many more students, the professors who teach them report greater numbers underprepared for college work. The evidence supports these impressions.[3] Less than one-half of high school graduates complete even a minimally defined college preparatory curriculum in high school, leaving colleges to remedy the educational gaps. Easy courses, poor counseling, and low expectations of students and teachers alike contribute to the mismatch between high school graduation and college readiness. For a student who falls behind at any time from primary through secondary school, few programs or strategies are on hand to help. Through a vicious downward cycle of lowered expectations, the student is all-to-quickly assigned to a general studies track, which leads neither to college preparation, nor to a career.

Surveys show that only four in ten high school teachers believe all students to be capable of success in a rigorous course of study.[16] With those responsible for public education holding such low expectations, it is small wonder that many students are underprepared for college. And yet, prepared or not, most high school graduates continue their studies.

The situation at the turn of the twenty-first century, with college education fast becoming the national standard, recalls the early twentieth century when the U.S. reached for universal high school attendance. In that moment of transition, the country discussed whether all students should get the same high school curriculum or be slotted into tracks seen as appropriate to their prospects. While many urged equal educational opportunities for all, tracking became the norm in public schools. More recently, the country began dismantling this inequitable pattern. While tracking may permit customized education for some students, it shuts off options for others, often unfavorably affecting racial minorities and the economically disadvantaged.[17] Even today, too many students still receive what Robert P. Moses calls "a ghetto education."[18]

It is society's responsibility to ensure all students powerful learning that prepares not only for a job, but for career advancement and a fulfilling life as well. Without this commitment, individual students and the broader community are shortchanged. If colleges hold low expectations for many of their students and shunt them into narrow or shallow tracks, they could be recreating at the collegiate level the severe, discriminatory problems of the twentieth-century high school experiment. As college education now becomes commonplace, all students must have the opportunity to achieve the most empowering forms of learning.

Expectations for greater success are not utopian dreams. Research confirms that when much is expected, much is achieved.[19] Similarly, low expectations lead to disappointing results. Raising expectations, however, means confronting the common perception that native ability counts more than hard work. While in some cultures parents teach their

INFORMATION

How the U.S. Reached Near-Universal College Attendance

Between 1960 and 2001, college enrollments expanded from 4.1 million to 14.8 million,[20] fueled by:

- a 57 percent increase in the U.S. population and the coming-of-age of the baby boom generation[21]
- a large growth of state college and university systems, including 743 new community colleges[22]
- the GI bills after the Korean and Vietnam wars that enabled 6.3 million veterans to attend college[23]
- 1964 civil rights legislation and Affirmative Action that helped expand minority student enrollment
- the Economic Opportunity Act of 1964 that established work-study
- a three-fold increase in federal support, including funds for loans, grants, teacher training, and infrastructure[24]
- attention to women's rights, the coeducation of many campuses, and Title IX legislation
- new opportunities for adult education, including distance learning
- recent pressure from the job market with newly invented jobs requiring a higher level of education to use technology and information.

Texas School District's Greater Expectations

In 1998, the BRAZOSPORT INDEPENDENT SCHOOL DISTRICT won the Texas Quality Award for dramatic improvements in learning across all groups. Of 13,500 students, approximately 9 percent are African American, 33 percent Hispanic, and 36 percent poor.

Adopting the belief that all students can learn at high levels, the district improved instruction to include enrichment and tutorials to reteach material if necessary.

While 1992 state-test pass rates for minority students were 20 to 30 percent lower than for white students, by 1999, all groups had improved, and 92 to 98 percent passed. So successful was the program, that the district reached student achievement goals two years ahead of projections.[26]

children to apply themselves or risk failure, Americans tend to attribute failure to a lack of talent.[25] When parents or teachers say, "Becky just can't do math," Becky gets the message she is not smart and feels helpless to do better. While nearly everyone admits that some people learn faster than others, too few know about the successes of exemplary schools and colleges across the country. These models of excellence—in urban, rural, and suburban settings—demonstrate how persistence, good teaching, and an environment of greater expectations can combine to elicit better performance from all students.

Our nation goes to college because ...

THE WORLD IS COMPLEX, INTERCONNECTED, AND MORE RELIANT ON KNOWLEDGE THAN EVER BEFORE. College has become a virtual necessity for individuals to build satisfying lives and careers. In a world of turbulent changes, every kind of occupation has seen a dramatic increase in education requirements. The majority of jobs considered desirable are now held by people with at least some college, and jobs for the best educated workers are growing the fastest.[27] The most attractive jobs and careers in the near future will require higher levels of education than in the past. Moreover, the explosion of readily available information means that being able to find out what one needs to know has begun to replace knowledge itself as an educated person's hallmark. Revolutionary technologies have transformed information and life. Changes succeed one another with increasing rapidity, so the need for people who can make sense of change is bound to continue.

Preparation for a fulfilling life, as well as a rewarding career, comprehends learning about the world, culture, and the arts. College education offers an understanding of the past, concepts for grappling with fundamental human and scientific questions, and tools to continue learning throughout life. It provides choices and a measure of control for negotiating a fluid and often stressful world. All these professional and personal benefits of college define it as an individual or private good.

College education also has important benefits for society. One public good is certainly economic. At this moment, even with more students in college, there is a looming shortage of exactly the employees needed by the knowledge-based economy: college educated people with mental agility and adaptability. Employers view the production of creative and intellectually skilled workers as essential for the country's prosperity in a competitive world. Producing this highly educated workforce depends on more students completing rigorous high school and college-level study.

The contribution of college education to a civic society is another public good. A democracy's success flows directly from the thoughtful participation of an informed citizenry. When people are well educated, they tend to participate more in their communities and to vote.[28] They acquire the tools and background to stay abreast of complex social issues. Knowledgeable, empathetic members of society help ensure enlightened policy decisions. The tragic events of September 11, 2001, renewed interest in education's responsibility to produce ethical and compassionate graduates, courageous enough to act on their convictions and reflective in shaping society's larger values.

September 11 also jolted Americans into recognizing the interdependence of the globe and the impossibility of any country to exist in isolation. Telecommunications, the ease of travel, and nuclear power, to name just a few developments, make everyone a global citizen. The largest multinational companies are like corporate states, with economies surpassing those of many countries and with worldwide power to match. Resolving issues affecting all of humankind—issues such as environmental pollution and pandemics—requires international cooperation. Of course, such collective action depends on individuals educated about the issues, but it also relies on skilled cross-cultural communicators and negotiators. As problems grow in scale and impact, so does the need for sophisticated cultural understanding. So, too, does U.S. responsibility for contributing its share of bi- or multi-linguists to global conversations. Preparing this globally competent populace is another public good of college.

These myriad private and public benefits of higher learning form the basis for a strong democracy, a healthy society, and, ultimately, a more peaceful world. They explain why, both for individual and societal reasons, everybody should have access to an excellent college education.

INFORMATION

Jobs and Education

87 percent of "elite job" holders and 53 percent of "good job" holders have more than a high school education.

From 1973 to 1998, the percentage of managers and business professionals with only a high school diploma fell by nearly 50 percent while those with at least some college rose substantially.

From 1998 to 2008, 14.1 million new jobs will require a bachelor's degree or at least some postsecondary education, more than double those requiring high school level skills or below.[29]

College graduates earn 80 percent more than high school graduates or $1,000,000 over a lifetime.[30]

Pressures on Higher Education

To summarize the analysis in this report, and other pressures outside its scope, higher education for the twenty-first century faces:

Changing demographics of college attendance	■ higher proportion of high school graduates ■ students lacking recommended college preparatory curricula ■ greater percentage of non-traditional students ■ more cultural diversity with higher minority participation
New enrollment patterns	■ increased part-time enrollment ■ multiple-institution attendance ■ online and distance courses
The information explosion	■ huge and rapidly increasing quantity of information widely available ■ looser review and control of information quality ■ shift from remembering facts to finding and evaluating information
The technological revolution	■ new types of jobs for graduates ■ changed nature of the classroom because of online learning
A stricter regulatory environment	■ greater call for accountability ■ more intrusive state regulation of the curriculum ■ in many states, the potential to expand from K-12 to college the strict standards and mandates that stress factual recall in testing ■ accreditation emphasis on effectiveness and assessment
New educational sites and formats	■ rapid growth in the for-profit higher education sector, with little regulation and accreditation ■ rise of the corporate university ■ more flexible learning formats
The changing nature of the workplace	■ emphasis on creative problem solving, team work, and adaptability ■ need for high-level intellectual skills ■ demand for large numbers of technologically and quantitatively literate employees ■ interaction with greater diversity of people
The global nature of major problems, requiring enhanced international cooperation	■ porosity of national boundaries ■ worldwide environmental impacts ■ multinational corporations ■ post 9/11/01 awareness of global interdependency
Renewed emphasis on civic responsibility and the development of communal values	■ rise in student volunteerism ■ cyclical student activism ■ increased pressure on colleges and universities to join the community in resolving local problems
Decreased state funding for public colleges and universities	

Pressures on Secondary Education

To summarize issues largely beyond the scope of this report, secondary education for the twenty-first century faces:

Changing demographics	■ growth in school-age minority population ■ increased numbers of immigrant students and those not proficient in English ■ ongoing achievement gaps for minority and economically disadvantaged students
New accountability demands	■ standards-based approach to learning, disconnected from how teachers are trained ■ demand for better qualified teachers, without corresponding financial support or incentives ■ college preparation needs misaligned with high school curricula and assessment
Changing educational policies and practices	■ requirements for evidence-based instructional practices ■ insufficient political will for adequate funding ■ vouchers, charter schools, and other alternatives to public education
Over-reliance on educational traditions	■ credit awarded for seat time rather than demonstrated competence ■ ongoing use of "social promotion" ■ school year based on an agrarian economy ■ assessments uncoupled from instructional changes to improve learning

We expect college to be ...

A CHALLENGING, LIFE-ENHANCING EXPERIENCE, with sophisticated, useful outcomes resulting from study and earning a degree. Those are the high expectations many in the U.S. hold for college education. This much seems to be agreed. However, at a more specific level, interested parties—students, families, employers, policymakers, educators, and the general public—hold divergent views about the purposes of college. These differences need to be addressed if the U.S. is to reap the potential benefits of expanded access.

Students: In the eyes of many students, whether traditional age or older adults, the college degree is the ticket to a good job. Some focus short-term on their first appointment, and others on the longer-term promise of white-collar employment and at least a middle class lifestyle. In choosing a college—largely by academic reputation[31]—students expect job-related courses that will well prepare them to enter or change to their chosen careers, and then advance within them.

Employers: Employers focus on the specific abilities they need in their employees. They expect colleges to graduate students able to perform consistently well, communicate effectively, think analytically, help solve problems, work collegially in diverse teams, and use relevant skills of the profession.[32] Increasingly, they expect technological and information literacy, and the private sector, in particular, looks for strong quantitative reasoning. Inconsistent results lead employers to question higher education's effectiveness and wish that its degrees, like technical certification, ensured documented levels of accomplishment.

Policymakers: Policymakers would like to see colleges and universities produce enough highly skilled graduates to satisfy workforce needs, but also to attract business and industry to local regions. They look for economic growth and improvements in statewide standards of living. As the demand for information- and technology-literate graduates (among others) is left unmet, higher education appears to be disengaged from many of these important societal needs.

The faculty: Ask college faculty members, and most will explain their hope for students to engage intellectually and seriously with what is

---

INFORMATION

Time-on-Task: Faculty and Student Expectations

Faculty members expect students to spend significant time preparing for their courses: the standard is generally two to three hours per hour of classroom instruction. Students, however seldom meet that standard; they generally believe that one hour per hour of class time is adequate.[33]

taught. Deep learning, they believe, develops the ability to defend positions based on knowledge, rather than simply on opinions. Professors expect students to write well and think clearly, explore multiple fields and modes of inquiry, and gain substantive knowledge in a particular field. As they see it, college learning should result in rational and reflective minds, open to continuous learning throughout a lifetime. The higher education community as a whole expects its members, both professors and students, to support free discussion that respects a variety of viewpoints, and to embrace the active life of the mind.

The public: While it recognizes vast differences in prestige among colleges, the general public expects quality and empowering education from them all. Whether graduating from community or liberal arts colleges, or from comprehensive or research universities, students are expected to be better at thinking and at knowledge-based work than after high school. The public anticipates that attendance will pay off in a more successful career, family life, and place in society. And although some important segments of society look for college graduates to assume leadership roles in the community, public attention focuses primarily on "getting in" to college, paying the bills, and then "getting out" with a degree. The public knows comparatively little about what actually happens during the college years.

Thus, while everyone expects college students to learn at high levels, each group tends to have a different view of what that implies. Some see the personal rewards, others the societal benefits. Some stress economic success, others intellectual vitality.

The Greater Expectations National Panel believes that a deepened understanding of the purposes of college for the twenty-first century can bring together these divergent expectations. Through this report and the New Academy it describes, the panel proposes a comprehensive vision of college learning, a vision that acknowledges the multiple purposes of higher learning in a complex society.

INFORMATION

Public Expectations

While 87 percent of the general public agree that a college education is as necessary as a high school diploma used to be, only 63 percent believe it essential for college to improve students' ability to solve problems and think analytically.

Even fewer, 57 percent, identify top-notch writing and speaking skills as essential outcomes of a collegiate education.

No more than 44 percent view active citizenship (for example voting and volunteering), as an essential college outcome.[34]

However two-thirds of U.S. voters believe it is very important for higher education to prepare people to function in a more diverse society and work force.[35]

Employers tend to expect more. Is there a need to educate the public better?

To preview the vision ...

WHAT INDIVIDUALS AND SOCIETY NEED is an invigorated liberal
education that expands horizons while nourishing the mind. Such an
education develops practical competencies so students can make a
difference in the world. By holding every student to high standards of
accomplishment, and supporting them all in meeting greater expectations,
this education will prove personally empowering, intellectually challenging, beneficial to civic society, and eminently useful. ■

CHAPTER 2

BARRIERS TO QUALITY FROM SCHOOL THROUGH COLLEGE

We have made great strides in opening the doors to college, but . . .

THE JOB IS NOT YET DONE AND ACCESS ALONE IS NOT ENOUGH. While near-universal college entrance represents a remarkable accomplishment and one in which to take great pride, students need both to complete college and to get from it a powerful education. At the heart of the Greater Expectations vision is the belief that everyone is entitled to an education of quality. To provide this opportunity, national priorities must change. They must shift from the recent focus on access alone, to the dual goals of:

- access to college learning of *high quality* for every student in the country, and
- appropriate preparation for all to *succeed* at this demanding level.

Neither goal can stand alone, nor will achievement of only one produce the changes needed. Each individual student, and the nation as a whole, is poorly served by an inequitable situation in which some receive second-class learning (or worse) in primary school, secondary school, or in college.

Formidable barriers stand in the way. Many who enter college must spend much of the first year catching up, particularly in mathematics and writing. Even then, between 40 and 60 percent do not finish a degree.[36] Great Britain, Finland, the Netherlands, and New Zealand now have higher college graduation rates than the United States.[37] Most worrying of all for a strong democracy is the continuing differential impact on minority groups and the economically disadvantaged, who disproportionately need remedial courses and leave college before completing their degrees.

In the Wake of *A Nation at Risk*

The 1983 report, *A Nation at Risk*,[38] proposed strengthening high school graduation requirements to include:

- four years of English
- three years of mathematics
- three years of science
- three years of social studies
- one-half year of computer science
- two years of foreign language (for college-bound students).

Although ever-increasing numbers of high school graduates complete the recommended minimum core curriculum, by 1995, 53 percent still had not. With 75 percent of these graduates now enrolling in postsecondary study, this success rate is not good enough. Are the 1983 guidelines adequate to prepare students for college? What learning happens in those courses?

From conversations among educational leaders and policymakers, produce standards and assessments that focus on intellectual capacities and reflect the complex nature of learning and learning styles.

Barriers to Readiness

Although readiness refers to the preparation of all students for successful college-level learning, different sets of hurdles confront traditional age and older students. Eighteen to twenty-two-year-olds face:

Uneven preparation for independent, demanding college-level study. Despite nearly two decades of school reform triggered by the 1983 report *A Nation at Risk*, many high schools are unable to produce college-ready graduates. Reasons include poor quality teaching, low teacher and student expectations, large class size, weak curricula, and unconscionably poor resources. Some schools suffer from all these handicaps. Models for how to solve the problems of uneven preparation exist, but the will to replicate them broadly has not yet been mustered.

The continuing patterns of separation and discrimination. Students of color tend to be concentrated in schools with the poorest resources and lowest expectations. Their high school dropout rates exceed those of majority students, thereby limiting their potential for advanced study. This unfair situation jeopardizes the futures of minority students, as well as the country's ability to equitably produce a well-educated populace.

Limited interpretations of learning. Learning is more than the simple acquisition of discrete facts. As students progress through their education, the need for analysis and integration, as well as factual recall, increases. In high school and college, students need to know facts, but even more importantly how to interpret and what to do with those facts. Information is transformed into internal knowledge as students apply their understandings to new situations, new problems, and new environments, thereby using their previous learning in challenging ways.

Learning is also more than the completion of a fixed number of courses. Some states have tried to create uniform high school graduation standards by establishing a minimum number of years for study in core subjects. Such standards measure only time spent, not the work performed, level of instruction, or, ultimately, learning attained.

A "one-size-fits-all" approach to assessment and to learning. State-mandated assessments at various levels from kindergarten through grade twelve can be equally problematic. In many states, the standardized testing movement is reinforcing the interpretation of learning as mere acquisition of unconnected facts, rather than correcting this impoverished view. Multiple choice tests, in particular, provide little evidence of the analytical power, creativity, resourcefulness, empathy, and abilities to apply knowledge and transfer skills from one environment to another that students will need for college success.[39] Moreover, the obsession with testing is diverting attention from comprehensive reforms of the curriculum and teaching that should be the highest priorities. When tests carry high stakes — when they determine whether students advance or graduate — teachers find themselves pressed to produce good results and thus learn to "teach to the tests," even if classroom dynamics suggest a different pace or approach.

Today's primary and secondary school students bring diverse learning styles to the classroom. They learn at different rates, in different ways, starting from different points, and with different levels of parental involvement. Yet, by and large, educators assume they will all fit into one standard pattern. While excellent teachers employ a range of instructional methods to match their students' learning styles, such master teachers are not available in all schools. Schools also are organized so that a set quantity of learning is expected in a given time frame. In only a few exceptional schools are all students held to high standards by adjusting both the kind and amount of instruction to meet individual student learning needs.

The misalignment of high school work with college entry expectations. Most colleges do not share with secondary schools what they expect incoming first-year students to know and be able to do to succeed in college. Nor do they make clear to college-bound students why the expected preparation matters. There is also a growing disconnect between the superficial "coverage" of survey courses that still predominate in high schools and an emerging emphasis on in-depth, investigative learning as early as the first year of college.

STORY

Good Learning at Landmark High

A small public school in New York City, LANDMARK HIGH SCHOOL serves a predominantly poor, Dominican population often left behind by education. But everyone at Landmark takes pride in its achievements: fewer than 2 percent of students drop out of school, and most graduates attend college.

According to former Principal Paul Schwarz, success can be attributed to two factors: small size and the collective responsibility of teachers and staff for everything that happens at Landmark. Also, linking rigorous, well-constructed performance assessment to both instruction and school improvement permits Landmark to focus on setting high standards. "We look at students' work and ask ourselves 'Is this what we mean by good work at Landmark? How can we make it better?'"

To graduate, students must build rich portfolios that demonstrate vital competencies. When asked about the portfolios, one student replied, "We just finished a course at John Jay College and had to do an 8-page term paper. Then we realized how much we had learned about research and writing by doing portfolios and how proud we are of our work."[40]

Occasionally, graduation can be held up by an unacceptable portfolio. If extra time is needed, the student is individually advised and helped to develop a plan for completion.

This situation of unstated and mismatched expectations may be left over from the time when colleges could more realistically assume a common background and preparation among the smaller group of entering students. Since this homogeneity is no longer the case, clear language from colleges about what they expect could greatly assist students and their counselors in selecting appropriate college preparatory courses. Toward what level of accomplishment in core subjects and in the intellectual skills important to many fields (such as oral communication or numerical literacy) should college aspirants strive?

The chaotic borderland between school and college. A range of formal curricular structures sit at the interface between high school and college. So-called college-level courses in high school (advanced placement, dual high school/college enrollment) are designed to accelerate engagement with college material. Sometimes, the level of learning taking place in these courses is unclear beyond coverage of certain content. Do students discuss and analyze at a college level? Are their writing assignments challenging? Are they learning research skills? In some schools, the frantic accumulation of AP credits for college applications breeds cynicism about their value, even among the strongest, most successful students. Other structures—courses in college that teach high school-level content—remedy gaps in prior preparation. While these arrangements on both sides of the high school-college border can serve students well, they tend to operate as isolated stepping stones, rather than as a true bridge between levels of learning. In the absence of clear and widely accepted educational principles about what counts as college-level learning, these borderland courses compound the confusion about college readiness.

ACTION STEPS

Create a mechanism to coordinate advanced placement, dual enrollment, and remedial college courses.

Expect high school seniors to complete a substantial, integrative piece of independent work to demonstrate their readiness for college-level work.

The wasted senior year. The senior year of high school should ideally be a time for students to undertake work approaching, in nature and level, that expected in the first year of college. It should be a time to synthesize, integrate, and demonstrate the learning of the previous eleven years. For many students, however, the reality is quite different. For them, the senior year means rather a waste of time and a loss of educational momentum, since the culture of low expectations for the senior year induces both high- and low-achieving students alike to slack off.[41] Many students, parents, and even some teachers view it as a time for students to relax and enjoy friends, before settling down to a job or to college. Meager state and district graduation requirements may allow seniors to carry a light course load if they have already met the minimum demands. High school exit exams, where they exist, may be taken as early as tenth grade in some regions, and can be passed with only ninth or tenth grade-level learning.

College admissions decisions largely rest on grades and SAT scores earned by the middle of senior year, and are rarely revoked even for lackluster second semester results. The early-decision option, recently more popular than ever, reinforces low senior year expectations for high achievers. By December, with college plans set, the top students have little incentive to work hard for the rest of the year. For all students, the damage done by the wasted senior year may be most evident in subjects like mathematics and foreign language, which are learned best through continuous study.

Interruption in the practice of being a student: Older adults starting or resuming college encounter some of the same barriers to readiness as do students straight from high school, but they may also need to readjust to the demands of formal study. These non-traditional students can find their prior academic learning out-of-date or forgotten. Entire fields previously studied may have mutated beyond recognition, or new ones arisen to take their place. Those students who stopped or dropped-out because of poor performance can face a crisis of confidence in their ability to succeed in learning. Adults may need transition courses to update their academic skills and connect their current goals with the expectations of their college or university.

Barriers to high quality

Preparing all students to succeed in college is one greater expectation. The other is to provide them all access to a learning experience of high quality. Here, too, important barriers exist.

The fragmentation of the curriculum. The structure of U.S. higher education was not designed to accommodate the large numbers of students who now go to college, their diversity, or their fluid and seemingly

---

STORY

College Admissions— A Tale of Three Students

Ben, Anita, and Sophie all attended an international high school. Ben's early admission to a U.S. college allowed him to work only the minimum during senior year. His grades dropped significantly, but the college still welcomed him.

Anita and Sophie applied to a prestigious British university. Both received offers of acceptance based on the expectation of their achieving top scores on the exit exams of their International Baccalaureate high school program. Given at the very end of senior year, the exams kept Anita studying intensively through May to ensure excellent performance. She passed with flying colors and attended the university of her choice. Sophie, influenced by Ben, studied less, failed to achieve the required scores, and saw her acceptance offer withdrawn.

ACTION STEPS

State and federal policy leaders and school boards provide sustained resources for universal readiness and college success.

chaotic attendance patterns. The shape of the undergraduate curriculum was essentially fixed half a century ago. It combines broad general education common to all students (usually completed in the first two years or out of sequence in later years), more specialized study (a major) to give deeper knowledge of a chosen field, and electives to suit students' individual interests. Although listed in the catalog as part of a curriculum, individual courses are effectively "owned" by departments, and most advanced courses by individual professors. Few faculty members teach to collectively owned goals. The student assembles an assortment of courses, each carrying a defined number of credits and assuming a standard time in class. The degree certifies completion of a fixed number of these often disconnected fragments. There is little internal coherence in curricula or programs, and even less a plan for connected learning. In 1985 the Association of American Colleges report, *Integrity in the College Curriculum,* concluded, "As for what passes as a college curriculum, almost anything goes."[42] This remains true on many campuses, and the advent of online courses, accessible from almost everywhere, is accelerating this fragmentation of learning.[43]

The organization of universities and colleges around disciplinary departments also hardened in a simpler time. In too many institutions, faculty members feel the strongest attachments to their disciplines, the weakest to the institution as a whole. The departmental structure reinforces the atomization of the curriculum by dividing knowledge into distinct fields, even though scholarship, learning, and life have no such artificial boundaries. Through faculty efforts to work across disciplines, multi-disciplinary approaches to learning have gained place and acceptance, altering the nature of the curriculum in the process. However, such integrative approaches still butt against real administrative problems and face formidable obstacles.

ACTION STEPS

Reform doctoral education so college professors are prepared to be effective educators as well as scholars.

Professors prepared as scholars not teachers. The dark secret of higher education is that most college professors are never trained to be teachers. As doctoral students, their dissertations demand research; teaching skills are assumed to be easy for intelligent people to acquire.[44] Interest in how learning occurs has remained largely confined to psychologists and schools of education. Colleges and universities reward gifted teaching, but rarely assist faculty members in any sustained way to become outstanding instructors. Contributions to teaching theory and practice through scholarly work often are not valued by a professor's institution or departmental colleagues. Academic reward processes (for annual raises, promotions, prestigious professorships) always include recognition of teaching excellence, but in many institutions—and not only the research universities—scholarship consistently outweighs it.

Exclusive definitions of quality. The definitions of a quality college education are still those of an earlier age. Institutions are rated by standards of exclusiveness and wealth, rather than how successfully their students learn. For the general public, and also for many educators, quality equates with prestige, and prestige with college ranking. Such published rankings include a mix of factors like the entering grades of freshmen, the percentage of applicants rejected, endowment size, faculty salaries, and the financial support from alumni. While the rankings report class size (an acknowledgment that small classes can enhance learning), reputation generally substitutes for college-wide measurement of student achievement.

Student success in learning is largely absent from national rankings, primarily because campuses have difficulty providing reliable, comparable data on how much and how well students learn. Prospective college applicants who look for outcome or value-added data from a campus are likely to be disappointed. The existing ranking arrangement values students' profiles at entry more than their accomplishments during the college years. Carried to its extreme, this interpretation of quality could mean a higher rating for a school that selectively accepts excellent high school students and teaches them nothing, than for a school that accepts mediocre students and teaches them a great deal. A campus interested in increasing its prestige will find more incentive to shift resources toward competitive admissions, for example, than to invest in practices known to improve learning.[45]

These criteria of excellence have another negative impact: they do little to encourage colleges and universities to create supportive learning climates

ACTION STEPS

Create and then implement a concept of rating and ranking colleges based on success in educating students that is flexible enough to suit a broad range of institutional missions.

for the diverse groups now in college. The spectrum of life experiences, ages, ethnicities, races, and worldviews in the contemporary classroom offers a way to learn through and with one another, leading all those involved toward better decisions.[46] This diversity-enriched learning has only recently entered into the definition of educational quality on campuses,[47] but still carries no weight in national rankings.

A dearth of meaningful assessment. By and large, colleges are unable to say with any certainty whether students have learned what the professors are teaching. This is particularly true of abilities like critical thinking that develop across the confines of individual courses. The absence of explicit descriptions of the outcomes desired hampers assessment. So, too, do the independent treatment of individual courses and faculty unfamiliarity with meaningful assessment methods. Without knowing how well students have learned, the faculty finds it difficult to improve education in any purposeful way. This lack of assessment data can frustrate the desire to lift performance expectations.

While complicating assessment, student mobility among institutions also heightens its importance. Multiple observations throughout a student's undergraduate career provide the best means of diagnosing weaknesses and taking corrective action.

The heavy financial burden on students. Federal and state financial aid programs, and state-supported public colleges and universities, have been crucial in opening the doors to college, but students themselves still carry a heavy economic load. Even among full-time students, nearly three-quarters work while attending college, most at least twenty-five hours per week. While often necessary to pay college costs, these jobs interfere with class schedules, course selection, and learning. Working students are less likely to graduate and even to finish their first year. Not unexpectedly, the vast majority of part-time students work at least a half-time job (approximately 77 percent).[48]

Demands of personal and family life. Many of today's older adult students balance family responsibilities with their courses. A mature seriousness about education can accompany their life-based experiences, but the

---

INFORMATION

The Working Full-time College Student

In 1999, 74 percent of full-time students worked while attending school, 46 percent of them at least twenty-five hours per week and 20 percent at least thirty-five hours per week.

---

63 percent of those who work at least twenty-five hours would not otherwise be able to attend college.

---

42 percent report that working hurts their grades, 53 percent that it limits their class schedules, 38 percent that it interferes with their choice of courses.

Unmet financial need at public, four-year institutions averages $3,800 for low-income and $3,000 for moderate-income students.[49]

needs of children, spouses, and elderly parents can cut into the time available for concentrated study.

Hope is on the horizon ...

DESPITE ALL THESE BARRIERS TO READINESS AND QUALITY.
The hope and optimism come from three directions:

- first, from the recognized past successes of U.S. higher education in serving the college-going population and society

- second, from recent great accomplishments in opening the doors of college to many more who wish to attend

- third, from the new creativity the National Panel has witnessed as faculty members across the country reinvent their own institution's practices for a contemporary education.

Through imaginative work at colleges and universities of every kind, a movement is already growing that points the way toward a new and more powerful vision of college learning. In spite of extensive barriers and the widely divergent expectations of various stakeholders, innovators on many campuses are mapping out a New Academy with the potential to serve the needs of this new student generation and of society. These innovators' dedication to students, to more integrated forms of learning, and to the noble profession of college teaching are already producing effective educational models that, taken together, provide a glimpse of the future—of a universal college education of high quality for the twenty-first century.

The academic world, however, as the repository of accumulated knowledge, functions as a conservator, slow to change in fundamental ways.[50] Thus, new ideas appear as pockets of innovation, taking root at the margins of institutions, and maintaining themselves by the patient effort of a few dedicated individuals. These innovations only slowly permeate the mainstream. Nevertheless, the National Panel has talked with leaders from dozens of campuses where promising approaches to undergraduate education can be found. Their stories throughout this report show the way of the future and offer real hope for change. And since U.S.

collegiate education evolved over time to produce a rich collection of institutions, each with its own distinctive mission and practices, the stories are drawn from many types of colleges and universities. This variety is an important strength, particularly in light of higher education's new mission to serve so many and such a range of students. As the academy embarks on needed reforms, care must be taken to preserve this multiplicity of approaches from efforts that would unwisely impose uniform solutions. ■

CHAPTER 3

THE LEARNING STUDENTS NEED FOR THE 21ST CENTURY

The education all students need ...

PREPARES THEM FOR PERSONAL SUCCESS AND FOSTERS A JUST, DEMOCRATIC SOCIETY. The panel believes that the elements of such an education can bring together the many expectations various groups hold for college study. The central question is simple: What should all students be learning in college? No matter their aspirations or prior preparation, what will all graduates require to lead personally fulfilling and socially responsible lives? What learning should result from an undergraduate education of quality, whether gained from study at a selective liberal arts college, an urban university, an open-enrollment community college for part-time adults, online courses, or a combination of them all?

Though easily framed, the question is not easily answered. By raising substantive issues, it looks for a response that goes far beyond a simple list of courses completed or books read.

The intentional learner

The panel recommends that colleges and universities place new emphasis on educating students to become intentional learners. In a turbulent and complex world, every college student will need to be purposeful and self-directed in multiple ways. Purpose implies clear goals, an understanding of process, and appropriate action. Further, purpose implies intention in one's actions. Becoming such an intentional learner means developing self-awareness about the reason for study, the learning process itself, and how education is used. Intentional learners are integrative thinkers who can see connections in seemingly disparate information and draw on a wide range of knowledge to make decisions. They adapt the skills learned in one situation to problems encountered in another: in a class-

STORY

Learning Goals Front and Center

At INDIANA UNIVERSITY-PURDUE UNIVERSITY, INDIANAPOLIS, the desired outcomes of college study are crystal clear. Six Principles for Undergraduate Learning summarize what graduates are expected to demonstrate, whether they major in the arts and sciences or in professional fields.

The principles are never far from anyone's mind, since the university has distributed thousands of laminated, three-hole punched copies for students and professors to slip into their notebooks.

room, the workplace, their communities, or their personal lives. As a result, intentional learners succeed even when instability is the only constant.

For intentional learners, intellectual study connects to personal life, formal education to work, and knowledge to social responsibility. Through understanding the power and implications of education, learners who are intentional consciously choose to act in ethical and responsible ways. Able to place themselves in the context of a diverse world, these learners draw on difference and commonality to produce a deeper experience of community.

The intentional learner is empowered through intellectual and practical skills

Mastery of a range of abilities and capacities empowers intentional learners as they maneuver in and shape a world in flux. The intellectual and practical skills needed are extensive, sophisticated, and expanding with the explosion of new technologies. As they progress through grades K-12 and the undergraduate years and at successively more challenging levels, empowered learners excel at:

- communicating in diverse settings and groups, using written, oral, and visual means, and in more than one language
- understanding and employing both quantitative and qualitative analysis to describe and solve problems
- interpreting, evaluating, and using information discerningly from a variety of sources
- integrating knowledge of various types and understanding complex systems
- resolving difficult issues creatively by employing multiple systems and tools
- deriving meaning from experience, as well as gathering information from observation
- transforming information into knowledge and knowledge into judgment and action
- demonstrating intellectual agility and managing change
- working well in teams, including those of diverse composition, and building consensus.

STORY

Developing Empowered Communicators

Learning to write well does not happen simply by taking a freshman English course. CORNELL UNIVERSITY understands that students need to practice their writing over and over again, in many contexts. Cornell's curriculum features "writing in the disciplines." At all levels and in virtually all areas of study, students use writing to learn, while they also learn to write. As one student reflected on his developing awareness of the writing process, "Writing within the context of history differs from what I have done in the past. We examined carefully how authors portrayed history ... the way in which they argued. This led me into first mimicking the type of argument ... and then toward arguments of my own."

The intentional learner is informed by knowledge and ways of knowing

Intentional learners possess a core of knowledge, both broad and deep, derived from many fields. Since study must be about something, the sophisticated cognitive skills developed by empowered learners cannot be separated from content knowledge. Higher education has traditionally sorted this knowledge into disciplines, each of which uses distinctive modes of inquiry that shape the way it sees the world. Self-aware, informed learners understand the value of multiple perspectives in gaining a complete picture. College education favors studying about significant, challenging issues as a way to hone intellectual and practical skills. Theories help explain phenomena, and the better informed learners become, the more precise their abilities to link theory with practice.

To become informed learners, students should have sustained opportunities, both in school and in college, to learn about:

- the human imagination, expression, and the products of many cultures
- the interrelations within and among global and cross-cultural communities
- means of modeling the natural, social, and technical worlds
- the values and histories underlying U.S. democracy.

The intentional learner is responsible for personal actions and civic values

Empowered and informed learners are also responsible. Through discussion, critical analysis, and introspection, they come to understand their roles in society and accept active participation. Open-minded and empathetic, responsible learners understand how abstract values relate to decisions in their lives. Responsible learners appreciate others, while also assuming accountability for themselves, their complex identities, and their conduct. By weaving moral reasoning into the social fabric of life and work, they help society shape its ethical values, and then live by those values.

To develop these competencies and commitments of responsible learners, education should foster:

- intellectual honesty and engagement in ongoing learning
- responsibility for society's moral health and for social justice
- active participation as a citizen of a diverse democracy
- respect for and appropriate use of intuition and feeling, as well as thinking
- discernment of consequences, including ethical consequences, of decisions and actions
- deep understanding of one's self and one's multiple identities that connect habits of mind, heart, and body
- respect for the complex identities of others, their histories, and their cultures.

The education all students need has been called ...

LIBERAL EDUCATION. Many of the characteristics of intentional, twenty-first century learners—empowered through the mastery of intellectual and practical skills, informed by knowledge, and responsible for their own and society's values—have a familiar ring. They recall the longstanding goals of college learning: developing the mind and intellect by engaging with important knowledge. An education with these goals has traditionally been called LIBERAL EDUCATION, liberal not in any political sense but in terms of opening and liberating the mind from ignorance.

The new educational vision this report advocates rests on the strength of liberal education. However, it brings a new shape to liberal education by assigning to it the capacity to develop mental agility, as well as intellectual power; a deep understanding of the world's variety, as well as a knowledge of Western culture; ethical action in the service of the individual and society, as well as critical judgment. As they participate in a knowledge-based economy and an increasingly interdependent world, all students will need to be nimble thinkers and creative problem solvers. To think outside the box, they will depend on intellectual flexibility, at least as much as on factual information. An ethical grounding and empathy for others will keep them centered in turbulent times.

Liberal education is an educational philosophy rather than a body of knowledge, specific courses, or type of institution. By drawing on a broad range of knowledge, it asks students to grapple with complicated, important issues, and usually expects them to learn at least one subject in greater depth and at an advanced level. Intellectual growth occurs as both broad and deep learning challenge previously held beliefs. The philosophy of liberal education depends less on particular subject matter than on an approach to teaching and learning. A student can prepare for a profession in a "liberal," mind-expanding manner, or study the humanities or social sciences (traditional "liberal arts" disciplines) narrowly and shallowly. Both small colleges and large universities can educate their students liberally, as can technical institutes; stories throughout this report provide examples.

The best undergraduate education for the twenty-first century will be based on a liberal education that produces an individual who is intentional about learning and life, empowered, informed, and responsible. To achieve these goals, liberal education will need to change in two major ways from its earlier incarnations. First, it must define itself as the best and most practical form of learning for a changing world and then strive to meet that standard. Second, it needs to become available to all students, not simply the self-selected (and comparatively privileged) group of the past. Such a liberal education, as the framework for the entire college experience, is not limited to selected disciplines or the introductory level. The aims of liberal education for the future can only be achieved when all parts of the educational experience, from high school through college, focus on them.

Reinvigorating liberal education by making it practical

Liberal education for the new century looks beyond the campus to the issues of society and the workplace. It aims to produce global thinkers. Quality liberal education prepares students for active participation in the private and public sectors, in a diverse democracy, and in an even more diverse global community. It has the strongest impact when studies reach beyond the classroom to the larger community, asking students to apply their developing analytical skills and ethical judgment to concrete

---

INFORMATION

Often Confused Terms

LIBERAL EDUCATION: A philosophy of education that empowers individuals, liberates the mind from ignorance, and cultivates social responsibility. Characterized by challenging encounters with important issues, and more a way of studying than specific content, liberal education can occur at all types of colleges and universities. "General education" (see below) and an expectation of in-depth study in at least one field normally comprise liberal education.

LIBERAL ARTS: Specific disciplines (the humanities, social sciences, and sciences).

LIBERAL ARTS COLLEGES: A particular institutional type—often small, often residential—that facilitates close interaction between faculty and students, while grounding its curriculum in the liberal arts disciplines.

ARTES LIBERALES: Historically, the basis for the modern liberal arts; the quadrivium (arithmetic, geometry, astronomy, and music) and the trivium (grammar, logic, and rhetoric).

GENERAL EDUCATION: The part of a liberal education curriculum shared by all students. It provides broad exposure to multiple disciplines and forms the basis for developing important intellectual and civic capacities. General education can take many different forms.

problems in the world around them, and to connect theory with the insights gained from practice.

This approach to liberal education—already visible on many campuses—erases the artificial distinctions between studies deemed liberal (interpreted to mean that they are not related to job training) and those called practical (which are assumed to be). A liberal education *is* a practical education because it develops just those capacities needed by every thinking adult: analytical skills, effective communication, practical intelligence, ethical judgment, and social responsibility. By expecting students to collaborate productively with people who are unlike them, a liberal education strengthens interpersonal skills useful in the workplace and community life. In fact, for much of its history, liberal education was recognized as practical, since it prepared society's civic and religious leaders for their professions. Many contemporary colleges and universities have maintained this emphasis of service to society (as in some church-affiliated or historically black institutions, or in U.S. military academies). The point, however, is that liberal education must reclaim this pragmatism and become consciously, intentionally pragmatic, while it remains conceptually rigorous; its test will be in the effectiveness of graduates to use knowledge thoughtfully in the wider world. Liberal education anchors the practical in the theoretical, as it develops in students important, sophisticated skills and intellectual capacities.

The new practical liberal education, in addition to developing the important capacities of communication and reason, also empowers those who possess it. Graduates with this kind of liberal education will have gained high level abilities, transferable from discipline to discipline and from one environment to another. By knowing the lessons of the past, possessing the ability to hear others in their own languages, and demonstrating an impressive toolbox of skills, graduates will look toward the future prepared for whatever arises. They will be flexible employees, as fields not yet imagined emerge. Their education will meet their own expectations, as well as those of their parents, teachers, employers, and civic leaders.

STORY

A Practical Liberal Education

The students at METROPOLITAN COLLEGE OF NEW YORK (formerly Audrey Cohen College) are mostly minority adults. They hold jobs, study full-time, and carry out self-designed "constructive action" projects every semester in their work environments. This unique model of education allows students to integrate theory, practice, and the study of society as they succeed in internships, jobs, and community service. While preparing for careers in business and human services, students also reflect every semester on the implications of ethical theory for the life of a professional. This transformative education raises students' expectations of themselves, thereby encouraging many to pursue graduate studies.

Embracing the practical dimensions of liberal education helps reconcile the divergent expectations of college. Yes, a reinvigorated liberal education expands horizons and develops intellectual skills. Yes, it shares knowledge and nurtures curiosity. But it also creates an educated citizenry and prepares students for good jobs, as well as for satisfying careers. It builds the competent workforce for local economies and a knowledge-based world. None of these outcomes are mutually exclusive. Rather, they reinforce one another to create of liberal education the best answer to the question: What is the learning all students need for the twenty-first century?

Reinvigorating liberal education by making it more inclusive

Liberal or liberating education has traditionally been the country's way of preparing its leaders. By developing their capacities to reason and critically evaluate, a liberal education readies them to decide important questions. By fostering a sense of social responsibility, it builds capacities to reach decisions that are wise and just.

Reasoned, wise decision-making continues as an important outcome of collegiate study. However, in this new century, shifting roles and greater collaboration will require all people at times to be leaders and at other times to be skilled followers. As leadership mutates into a more nuanced, dynamic concept, the benefits of a liberal education will be valuable— even invaluable—for everyone. Fortunately, the near-universality of college study is making this ideal a real possibility. Even those who have been forced to struggle first for their freedom and then for inclusion, can now look forward to the liberating power of liberal education.

The true benefits arise, however, not merely by letting everyone in. In its very essence, liberal education for the twenty-first century is diverse and inclusive in every way. It seeks out varied perspectives, crosses disciplinary lines, pursues wisdom from multiple cultures, and employs a range of teaching strategies. It occurs in all types of institutions, not just elite colleges. It is powerful for all students, those studying traditional

ACTION STEPS

College and university leaders, business leaders, national associations, students, and parents initiate, participate in, and sustain public dialogues about the goals of a contemporary liberal education and how they serve individuals and society.

STORY

Preparation for a Changing World

Early one morning a few years ago, while waiting at the airport, the president of a major state university was greeted cheerfully by a new graduate. In response to a question about how and what he was doing, this recent alumnus described his work at a software company. He explained how the firm itself had not existed when he started college four years earlier, nor had its line of business. In following up this conversation, the president asked engineering faculty members how they prepared students for a world that is changing so rapidly. "By teaching them how to think and learn," they replied. Not at all a bad answer.

INFORMATION

A CEO Speaks Out for Liberal Education

Referring to the competitive, global nature of business, former Xerox CEO David T. Kearns remarked:

In such a world there is only one constant: change. And the only education that prepares us for change is a liberal education. In periods of change, narrow specialization condemns us to inflexibility—precisely what we do not need. We need the flexible intellectual tools to be problem solvers, to be able to continue learning over time… [I]t is not simply what you know that counts, but the ability to use what you know. In this way knowledge is power— the ability to use specialized knowledge as you adapt to new requirements.[51]

arts and sciences disciplines and those in professional programs. Finally, it calls for high standards, but without imposing standardized solutions. The enriched learning environment created by this diversity is essential to preparing all students for the challenges ahead. Education's responsibility to society demands no less.

The goal of liberal education remains success in powerful, quality learning, not merely access to a college degree. The nation's colleges and universities already utilize some promising practices to ensure quality learning for all students. But because preparation for liberal education begins long before students reach college, achieving the quality and inclusiveness desired in the New Academy will take concerted and collaborative action across education levels. All those with a stake in higher education will need to accept their individual and joint responsibilities. ■

PRINCIPLES OF GOOD PRACTICE IN THE NEW ACADEMY

Learning Goals across the Curriculum

DUKE UNIVERSITY'S Curriculum 2000 provides innovative, inquiry-based liberal education. Through multiple experiences across courses and semesters, students achieve general learning goals. While completing courses in required areas of knowledge, students simultaneously develop designated competencies (like writing), use modes of inquiry (like deductive reasoning), and engage with selected themes (like science and society). Creative combinations may occur, such as applying quantitative skills in a humanities course.

ACTION STEPS

Each college and university sets explicit goals for student learning so academic department and general education outcomes can align with them.

Campus leaders place their institution's vision of liberal education at the center of strategic planning efforts and resource allocation.

We can reach the goals by ...

MODELING SELF-AWARENESS AND A CLEAR SENSE OF EDUCATIONAL PURPOSE. The goals are now clear: universal student access to and readiness for an empowering liberal education that prepares for life, work, and citizenship in the twenty-first century. How can these goals be reached? Pieces of the answer are in place on many college and university campuses and they point the way forward toward the New Academy, centered on learning. The next step in assembling these pieces into a systematic and systemic movement for change depends on many campuses examining how well their practices help students learn. Are they role models for the self-reflection and purposeful action—the intentionality—expected of students? Do their curricula, teaching, advising, and operations coordinate to encourage achievement of important learning goals? How seriously do they take their responsibility for educating all students well for an uncertain future?

Learning as the center

Teaching and learning may be intimately connected, but, as any student knows, they are not the same. Faculty members at all levels methodically identify what should be taught, but spend less time finding out what students have actually learned. With learning as the center, what students learn is of primary importance. Knowledge of how learning occurs is a resource to make it happen better. Since a diverse student body learns in equally varied ways, students learn from one another, as well as from their teachers, and, indeed, teachers also learn from their students: this mutuality characterizes a learning-centered education. Students are treated as individuals, but also as

Learning Communities

In learning communities, cohorts of students enroll in at least two linked courses that often involve close interactions among students and professors. At THE EVERGREEN STATE COLLEGE, learning communities constitute the foundation of all academic work. Most are multidisciplinary and team-taught. A single learning community may make up a student's entire course load and center on a compelling theme or question. Professors actively involve students in the learning process through off-campus activities integrated with classroom study. Annual redesigns keep the offerings fresh. While innovative, Evergreen's curriculum is funded within the constraints of the traditional state formula.

Curricular Coherence

The KING'S COLLEGE faculty have created a coherent curriculum based on seven transferable skills of liberal learning. Both general education and major courses integrate skills with subject matter. Students work on their skills repeatedly, in a planned sequence, throughout their undergraduate careers. Assessments embedded in courses and projects supply evidence of learning. Each department has discipline-specific objectives for the transferable skills and charts their development from the first year, through a sophomore/junior project, into major courses. A senior project provides a final, powerful integration of the skills, the major, and general education.

members of groups—multiple and often overlapping groups. Powerful learning is intentionally nurtured over time.

Focusing education on learning should not be a radical concept for schools and colleges. But, in fact, when taken seriously, it implies far-reaching changes. For example, college becomes most importantly a place where people learn, rather than where they teach. The value of the credit unit also comes into question. Do credits earned, which equate to time spent in class, really certify learning? Does sitting through and passing two three-credit courses mean a student can communicate well enough in a second language? If the triple goals of intellectual and practical skill mastery, knowledge gain, and personal responsibility growth are what count, shouldn't how long it takes to acquire them become secondary? With learning truly as the center of education, the current practice of fixing a constant time for learning could logically give way to a more flexible model in which students are allowed variable time to achieve the outcomes desired.

Just as time is seen differently in an education focused on learning, so, too, is place. Learning happens during formal classroom study, but also in other ways. So while two semesters may not produce competence in a second language, many other pathways might do so: a longer series of courses, living abroad, growing up in a bilingual family, or studying in an immersion environment. Likewise, leadership skills can grow by theoretical study, leading a group in class, holding office in the student government, or being captain of a sports team. With a stress on learning, a student's capacity or proficiency matters more than the subject matter taught, courses completed, or credits earned.

Coherent pathways for learning. Well-designed curricula are more than collections of independent courses; they are pathways for learning. Graduating intentional learners—empowered, informed, and responsible— calls for curricula designed to further learning goals in a sequential manner across all the college years. Goals for learning, transparent to students and professors, justify the curriculum's design. For instance, a course or module is required at a certain point because it introduces students to the essentials of information retrieval and evaluation, in preparation for subsequent courses that assign research papers.

Traditionally, collegiate practice has separated general education, study in the major, and electives from one another. Preprofessional education has stood off by itself, only tangentially linked to other college programs. Yet the complex capacities and knowledge desired in college graduates can develop through all the courses and non-course experiences of a student's college years. Some lay the groundwork for learning, others advance it to a higher level. Since students' advanced work occurs in the major area of concentration, that seems the logical site for the most demanding assignments: demanding in content knowledge of the field, but also in the broad intellectual capacities of an intentional learner. While economics majors may learn the basics of college-level writing in a freshman composition course, for example, they will also need to write well about economics; the same holds true for business students or physicists.

In the New Academy, curricula will integrate general education and study in the major, including preprofessional programs, so that they form a consistent whole. But this does not mean that all students will take a common set of courses or that such a common core would provide all the necessary integration. The goals of liberal education are so challenging that all the years of college and the entire curriculum are needed to accomplish them.[52] Responsibility for a coherent curriculum rests on the shoulders of all faculty members working cooperatively.

Student mobility makes the job of assuring coherence more difficult. However, most baccalaureate institutions require students to complete a certain number of credits at the home campus as part of the degree. This "curricular residency requirement," usually equal to the senior year, provides an opportunity for students themselves to find coherence in their learning. Just as high school seniors might be asked to complete a piece of independent work to demonstrate their abilities to colleges (and to external audiences), so, too, could college seniors during this residency period undertake a project or major piece of research. In such a capstone experience, that would vary in design from one field to another, students could draw on and provide evidence of their learning no matter where or how it had occurred.[53] Oversight of this final and summative work could then allow the degree-granting institution to

STORY

Mutually Enriching Liberal and Professional Study

The skills and abilities essential for a business professional are developed through both liberal arts and professional courses at BABSON COLLEGE. A new integrated curriculum challenges students to demonstrate core knowledge, skills, and attitudes while they learn in hands-on ways. In a foundational course student teams actually create, run, and dissolve a business, while also developing their communication and critical thinking skills. Complex historical and social issues raised in advanced liberal arts courses relate directly to increasingly difficult decision-making scenarios in upper-level management study.

ACTION STEPS

Colleges and universities implement curricula to develop student knowledge and intellectual capacities cumulatively and sequentially, drawing on all types of courses (general education, the major, electives) and non-course experiences.

Expect college seniors to complete an integrative capstone experience as evidence of advanced college-level learning.

STORY

Active Learning

Active learning in many forms motivates students at RENSSELAER POLYTECHNIC INSTITUTE, the STATE UNIVERSITY OF NEW YORK AT STONY BROOK, and the UNIVERSITY OF NEBRASKA-LINCOLN. At RPI, "studio classrooms" utilize cutting-edge technology and research-based teaching methods to allow students to complete challenging projects that intertwine classroom knowledge and application. At Stony Brook more than 41 percent of undergraduates now benefit from a research experience, often as early as the first year.[54] Through Nebraska's UCARE program, students have a two-year opportunity to do research, serving as an assistant the first year, while carrying out independent research projects in the second.

ACTION STEPS

College and university faculty members focus on important student outcomes, regularly assess student progress, base teaching on research about learning, and raise expectations of student achievement.

assess and certify a student's achievement to employers and society. A similar type of assignment might be used to document student learning for transfer from community colleges to universities.

Teaching for powerful learning. Methods of teaching largely determine what learning occurs. Individuals who are empowered and informed are likely to arise from teaching that uses intellectual skills within rich disciplinary and multidisciplinary contexts. Complex capacities like creativity and reflection are honed as students encounter knowledge in new contexts and open-ended or unscripted problems. A student's sense of how knowledge relates to life grows by grappling with untidy social questions.

Teaching for powerful learning uses a range of methods, so each student can work up to his or her potential. Individuals turn information into knowledge through a process of translation, but their styles of doing so can differ widely. For some people, it works better visually, for others aurally or conceptually, and for still others through first-hand experience. Both reading and hands-on work—doing research or art, performing music or drama, serving local community groups—can deepen knowledge. A mix of individual and collective classroom activities teaches about independence and about interdependence. Group projects nurture negotiation skills, conflict resolution, teamwork, collaboration, and a practical understanding of people from diverse backgrounds. Since no one discipline monopolizes particular learning outcomes, a powerful education repeatedly exposes students to multiple teaching methods across the curriculum. Technology-based instruction can supplement and complement more traditional methods, just as learning by doing can enrich learning from lectures. Effective teachers use scholarly work on motivating a class as a resource to improve performance.

Teaching to Create Intentional Learners—Selected Examples

The Empowered Learner

Outcome	Facilitating Strategies
communicate well in diverse settings and groups, using written and oral means	writing assignments of multiple kinds (expository, creative, and personal writing) for many purposes; required and critiqued oral presentations
employ a variety of skills to solve problems	problem-based learning; undergraduate research; inquiry-based science labs
work well in teams, including those of diverse composition, and build consensus	planned and supervised experiences in teamwork, both in class and in off-campus settings

The Informed Learner

Area of Knowledge	Facilitating Strategies
the human imagination, expression, and the products of many cultures	interdisciplinary and integrated courses on creativity through the ages
global and cross-cultural communities	drawing on students' diverse experiences to enrich classroom discussion; integrating study abroad into courses back on the home campus; teaching courses world-wide through video-conferencing
modeling the natural world	student team-designed lab experiments to answer questions

The Responsible Learner

Responsibility Expected	Facilitating Strategies
active participation as a citizen of a diverse democracy	service learning; debate on proposed solutions to current social problems
understanding oneself and one's multiple identities	personal writing that requires self-reflection upon a wide variety of subjects, and that situates the self in relation to others

STORY

Advising for Personalized Learning

At HAMPSHIRE COLLEGE, advising is key to students' navigation through an academic program that emphasizes both the exploration of deep interests and substantial work in the liberal arts. Professors offer advice, support, and constructive criticism, as students design an individual plan to progress through three designated developmental levels. Impressive academic, artistic, and scientific accomplishments result.

ACTION STEPS

Educators at every level develop robust academic advising systems to explain the high expectations of college-level learning and help students map coherent pathways through a landscape of many institutions and programs.

STORY

A College that Practices What it Preaches

COLGATE UNIVERSITY's firm commitment to the integration of knowledge finds its way into all faculty personnel processes. New faculty hires get written expectations for interdisciplinary work. Third year review, tenure, and promotion decisions depend, in part, on interdisciplinary contributions. All dossiers must document participation in the interdisciplinary core curriculum, whose director votes on promotion and tenure.

Advising to develop self-reliance. Students of the New Academy will be actively engaged with the process of their learning. The nearly 60 percent who move from college to college will profit most from assuming personal responsibility for assembling a coherent whole from disparate parts. The multiple institutions in which they enroll are unlikely do it for them. As these peripatetic students find their way through educational forests, they require figurative maps (the reasons for taking specific courses and their learning expectations) and map-reading skills. Many pathways may exist for reaching their goals. By understanding the topographical elements of the map and orienting themselves as to their starting points and desired ends, they can select appropriate routes. Teaching these map-reading and navigation skills is the job of advisors in this new learning-centered environment. Institutions define the topographical elements (explain the learning expected to result from their programs). However, greater student responsibility for charting a course through the learning process by no means relieves the faculty of its duty to design coherent curricula. Nor does it relieve the institutions themselves of the need to dismantle barriers standing in the way of connected and versatile learning. In fact, nation-wide solutions to cross-institutional advising, record keeping, and certification may evolve over time in the New Academy.

Practicing what it preaches: the intentional college or university. Colleges and universities of the New Academy will support curricula and teaching by strategic use of their resources. Building a culture centered on learning is the job of presidents and their senior staffs. Their commitment to reinvigorated liberal education guides the choice of faculty, programs, and directions. This institutional purpose, mirroring the intentionality of students and the coherence of the curriculum, builds on operations and systems aligned with the institution's mission. Curricular and cocurricular programs mutually reinforce one another. Both in continuing operations and times of special self-reflection—strategic planning, reaccreditation, capital campaigns—campuses keep their eyes on the prize.

Navigating in an Unfamiliar Land: Orienteering[55]

Orienteering Principles	Orienteering in Education
Orienteers use an accurate, detailed map and a compass to find points in the landscape.	Accurate, detailed "maps" of learning goals and curricula identify potential learning experiences. The "compasses" that point students toward goals are academic advisors, mentoring professors, and career information. Required proficiencies and assessments, often completed in a specific sequence, are educational "points in the landscape." Students attending multiple institutions need a portable compass that will guide them through inevitably more complex terrain.
Novices first go through a simple course and then progressively more difficult ones to learn map-reading skills.	Freshman experiences provide extended orientation to college life and learning. Some students may need specific remedial study to support their transition to college. Early successes are important for novice learners regardless of the topic. As in orienteering, some educational experiences will require close supervision by experts so no one gets lost. Both the difficulty of the task and the independence of the learner increase as the student moves to more advanced levels.
A standard orienteering course consists of a start, a series of sequentially numbered control sites, and a finish.	College learning is coherent and carefully sequenced. An advisor familiar with a student's goals and intended field(s) of study helps develop a personal plan for learning to guide progress even through multiple institutions and changes of the end goal.
The route between control points is not specified, but left entirely to the orienteer. Route choice and the ability to navigate through the forest are the essence of orienteering. Repeated experiences build expertise.	There may be many routes to a degree. Previous learning, cocurricular experiences, and personal abilities influence the choice of an advantageous route. Advising and the student's own growing expertise will be compasses pointing the way to a degree. Routes that are too indirect can carry a heavy cost for individuals and society in terms of time, money, and talent wasted.
Other aspects of orienteering include early experiences in learning to read maps and interpret map symbols, and learning about specialized equipment.	Pre-college information about colleges, degree programs, certifications, careers, and work will help to prepare students for their paths through postsecondary education. Learning to "read and interpret" information about schools and degree programs (including the vocabulary of advanced learning) contributes to student independence. Advisors must stay up-to-date on changes in educational "terrain" and "equipment" in order to ensure continued, accurate advising.

ACTION STEPS

Faculty members across disciplines and departments assume collective responsibility for the entire curriculum to ensure every student an enriching liberal education.

Faculty reward systems value learning-centered education.

Centers of teaching and learning on every campus make available significant resources to support faculty members as they assume the responsibilities of learning-centered education.

STORY

Supporting the Faculty to Improve Student Learning

Belief in the power of excellent teaching is strong at RICHLAND COLLEGE of the Dallas County Community College District. Comprehensive programs of faculty development focus on continuous improvement of teaching and learning. Each faculty and staff member proposes an annual plan for personal growth, related to student learning, that is used in performance evaluations.

With military personnel typically appointed to the faculty for only three years, preparing new professors has become a U.S. AIR FORCE ACADEMY specialty. Programs include a comprehensive orientation, frequent teaching improvement workshops, and observations of an excellent teacher shortly before a new faculty member teaches the same lesson.

All members of the campus community share language to describe its learning-centered culture. The institution's central purpose is evident in communications to prospective students and in presidential addresses. A diverse community, paired with an education that values the experiences of all individuals and groups, is central to the strategy.

Faculty members on a learning-centered campus make a collective commitment to high quality education. The concept of "my work," so characteristic of the present educational culture, becomes "our work," with the entire faculty assuming responsibility for the entire curriculum.[56] The "saying" and "doing" of the institution coincide, fostered by open conversation, joint action, and appropriate reward systems. In terms of its operations, the institution itself becomes a life-long learner, continuously evaluating and assessing itself at all levels, then feeding the results back into improvement loops for both student learning and campus processes.

In the transition period, as the new culture of learning-centered education expands, faculties will need assurance of the institution's serious commitment. Colleges and universities with learning as the center of their work provide professors with every means possible to teach, advise, and mentor their students well. User friendly and extensive programs of faculty development help them also become professional educators.

No one model of intentional operation applies to all colleges and universities. Quite the contrary. Various missions, cultures, histories, and student bodies shape a range of examples. While, in the New Academy, all campuses will have goals for the kind of learning students need (and the goals themselves may well be similar), the emphases, balance between them, and plan for their achievement might differ radically. Whereas all institutions will recognize the importance of evaluation and continuous improvement, local methods may be more effective than external, standardized ones. As in student learning, the overall hope is for high standards without standardization. The relevant metaphor is one of multiple paths winding up the mountain to greater student achievement.

We can bring students along by . . .

PREPARING THEM FOR COLLEGE, SINCE THE COLLEGE YEARS DO NOT STAND ALONE. Education neither begins nor ends with college, nor can the goal of ensuring high quality liberal education for all students be met by changes only in higher education. Since college attendance is now assumed, and it is less a question of if than when a student will enroll, high schools should prepare every graduate for post-secondary education. Clarity in what colleges expect of entering students and alignment of those expectations with high school graduation requirements are both essential parts of the solution; so, also, are producing excellent primary and secondary school teachers, building community understanding of quality education, and helping parents and spouses provide supportive environments.

More important than knowing simply what subjects students should study in preparation for college (although continuous study certainly counts) is knowing what they should, and actually do, learn. What knowledge stays with them? What intellectual skills can they demonstrate? Research indicates that rigorous high school work correlates with good college performance,[57] and rigor means both the sophistication of subject matter and the amount of effort required for success. High school classes, then, should be demanding in terms of both content and intellectual activity.

If high schools introduce students to the same kinds of learning they will encounter in college (such as using critical abilities to address complex issues drawn from real life), their graduates will be better prepared for the more advanced work of college. The varied teaching methods being called for in college can also serve the range of high school students' learning styles.

Currently the task of training elementary and secondary school teachers rests with departments and schools of education. Achieving greater expectations for all students spreads responsibility for teacher preparation across the entire college or university. Teachers themselves will need

STORY

Aligning High School and College Learning

Based on standards that describe the academic skills and knowledge students need to be accepted into Oregon's public universities, the PASS (PROFICIENCY-BASED ADMISSION STANDARDS SYSTEM) program features a portfolio of significant work to verify high school student achievement. The Oregon University System uses PASS data for placement in entry-level courses.[58]

Through STANDARDS FOR SUCCESS (S4S), selective research universities across the country are describing what knowledge and skills they desire in well-prepared entering students. The project also analyzes state educational standards and assessments at the high school level to determine their potential use in the admissions process.[59]

to be highly skilled in three ways:

- as professional educators, and therefore knowledgeable about learning and teaching
- in the disciplines they will teach, and therefore solidly grounded in content
- in the range of important intellectual abilities students in their classrooms will be expected to develop, thereby becoming themselves models of intentional learners—empowered, informed, and responsible.

The first capacity they will get through teacher education programs, the second by majoring in a disciplinary field, and the third by graduating from a rigorous liberal education program. Arts and sciences faculties in colleges and universities will be needed as engaged partners to assure the quality of liberal education for future teachers. It will be highly desirable for students of education to see in practice—in many disciplines—the varied and engaging teaching methods they may find useful in their own classrooms.

To this point, the discussion regarding preparation for college has been related to traditional students who come straight from high school. But many of today's students have interrupted their formal education for shorter or longer periods of time. These older students bring special perspectives into the classroom. For the colleges and universities serving non-traditional student populations, evaluating their preparation—formal and from life experiences—is increasing in importance as their numbers rise.

We can ensure ongoing improvement by ...

KNOWING HOW WELL STUDENTS ARE LEARNING. Evaluation of what individual students learn in courses has always been part of teaching. Faculty members review work and assign a grade. Traditional evaluation of this type is generally done well and conscientiously. Student dissatisfaction tends to arise when tests seem unrelated to the work of the course, either in content or testing style.

Much less often, however, do professors gather information about competencies that grow during an entire undergraduate career or about collective student performance (by aggregating individual results). While most colleges, for example, say that one of their goals is developing students' abilities in critical thinking, only a few determine how well the student body as a whole analyzes or synthesizes as seniors, much less as entering first-year students. Outsiders who find college graduates unprepared for solving problems in the workplace question whether the colleges are successfully educating their students to think; the colleges have difficulty proving their success.

Assessment is part and parcel of the teaching/learning process. Explicit goals—written and widely shared—specifying what students are expected to know, form the basis for assessment. Learning goals establish the foundation for aligning curricula, teaching, and assessment.

In a continuous manner, colleges should want to make sure that students are learning. Informal assessments conducted during a course (formative assessment) can help a teacher change direction in mid-stream if it appears that students have not understood well enough. More formal evaluation at the end (summative assessment) can feed back into shaping the course design itself. The more closely assessment methods or testing reflect classroom activities, the better they will point up strengths or weaknesses. For example, students expected to critically evaluate complex issues on a final exam need to be asked throughout the course to practice analysis.

Assessments at levels broader than the individual classroom require careful curricular planning. If a college expects all seniors to write convincingly as well as correctly, students will need to write for many courses, throughout the curriculum, over all their years of attendance. Since college educational aims comprehend many abilities that cut across individual courses, senior year assessments could ideally demonstrate skill in integrating a number of them. Portfolios of student work, including web-based portfolios, offer a potentially valuable assessment mechanism.

STORY

Evaluating Prior Learning

Students enter PACIFIC OAKS COLLEGE to finish their degrees. Those previously employed and with prior college credits, can opt to follow the Admission by Life Experiences program. ABLE—embodying in its name the college's self-affirming philosophy—helps them demonstrate how their life and work equate to college credit. Reflective examination of prior learning occurs in a semester-long formal seminar. Students develop theory to examine practice, thereby understanding better the assets they bring back to college. "The program boosted my self esteem and changed my goals," affirmed one ABLE graduate.

STORY

A Culture of Assessment

Assessment of learning begins as soon as students arrive at ALVERNO COLLEGE, when they complete diagnostic assessments to show their abilities. Results are used to design each student's academic program. Class work in disciplinary and interdisciplinary fields then focuses on eight general abilities at six levels of development. Criteria for assessment are public. Faculty members train volunteers from the community to serve as external evaluators. Students demonstrate their learning in multiple ways, such as public speaking, writing, lab work, and portfolio presentations. At Alverno, assessment of performance by teachers, peers, and students themselves is an integral part of the learning process.

Cumulative Assessment

Finding out how well students have learned involves assessment beyond the confines of a single course.

The students at WORCESTER POLYTECHNIC INSTITUTE expect to apply their knowledge; many are budding engineers. All must complete three demanding, hands-on projects, many done abroad and on questions of social consequence. Senior projects, often proposed by teams, solve significant theoretical or practical problems at the level of beginning professionals. Each project provides evidence of achievement—in technical fields, of broad abilities, and in integrating knowledge.

At PORTLAND STATE UNIVERSITY, a senior capstone in general education places student groups in communities to work on local projects. Students draw on learning from their majors and general education. The challenges faced in a diverse, urban setting require interdisciplinary thinking and teamwork. The capstone provides evidence of important personal and academic skills.

The use of traditional and digital portfolios has expanded as colleges look for evidence of complex learning. These collections of student work, assembled over time, can dramatically show student intellectual growth. Supported by The Pew Charitable Trusts, EASTERN NEW MEXICO UNIVERSITY and MOUNT ST. MARY'S COLLEGE (CA) have collaborated with others institutions to develop a model for digital portfolios. In addition to illustrating knowledge, the digital portfolios exemplify technological literacy.

So, too, do senior projects. To become a truly effective tool, a portfolio serves as more than a collection of student work, interesting as that may be; an evaluation of the learning demonstrated finds its way back into improved programs and teaching. As an example, if a sampling of seniors' portfolios indicated only an introductory ability to formulate hypotheses and test them, the faculty responsible would review where and how in the curriculum this aspect of critical thinking could be strengthened.

When taken seriously, assessment shapes curricula and instructional practice. The business community axiom that "what gets measured, gets done" holds true in education as well. If limited interpretations of assessment lead to external standardized tests that primarily evaluate the low-level skills of factual recall, classroom activities will focus on facts, rather than on understanding. A more nuanced interpretation of assessment recognizes that locally devised mechanisms, often embedded in coursework, can provide more relevant information. An "authentic assignment," similar to what an expert in the field might face, can serve to assess multiple types of learning, and do so at sophisticated levels. If, for example, students are expected to be learning about the history of civil rights, a multiple-choice test will show if they know the major issues, names of activists, and important dates. An assignment asking them to design a voter registration drive given a set of historical constraints could probe for a much deeper understanding of racial and ethnic cultures, while also assessing writing and analytical ability.

In the culture of the New Academy—a culture of evidence[60]—assessment is a necessary and integral part of greater student achievement. It becomes predominantly a tool for improvement: to improve learning, teaching, and the curriculum. Learning-centered assessment can be linked to courses and allow professors to answer for themselves the important questions of what, how much, and how well their students are learning. Assessment need not remain the threatening concept it often now seems to faculty members, identified with external control and infringement on academic freedom.

Assessment for improvement can have the added benefit of showing external stakeholders the academy's success in doing its job: educating students. Explicit learning goals and transparent assessment results could go a long way toward satisfying the demands for accountability and improved learning that are arising in many states. ■

ACTION STEPS

State and federal policy leaders, boards of trustees, and accrediting associations base institutional accountability on demonstrated student success in achieving liberal education outcomes.

STORY

Assessment and Accreditation

The associations that accredit institutions and professional programs believe strongly in the value of assessing student learning. New standards stress outcomes, performance, and improvement. In its revised handbook for institutional self-study, the MIDDLE STATES COMMISSION ON HIGHER EDUCATION looks for clear learning goals, coherent curricula, and their relationship to assessment.

A practical liberal education and preparation for professional careers share many important outcomes of college learning. Engineers need to work in teams and nurses to appreciate diversity. From conversations with regional and specialized accreditors, the GREATER EXPECTATIONS PROJECT ON ACCREDITATION AND ASSESSMENT identified the common expectations that can provide the basis for integrated, comprehensive assessment of learning, no matter what a student's major.[61]

Promoting Greater Expectations on Campus:
Starting Down the Path

1. Encourage broad conversations about greater expectations and learning-centered, twenty-first century liberal education; listen to many voices.

2. Develop a clear statement of functional goals for student learning, from entrance through graduation, and share those goals publicly (including with high schools).

3. Review strategic plans and resource allocation decisions for the centrality of learning within the mission of the institution.

4. Provide faculty and staff development about teaching, curriculum, assessment, collective responsibility, and collaborative leadership.

5. Begin to review the curriculum to ensure that its design supports student progress toward the goals.

6. Plan out the next five steps.

Chapter 5

Achieving Greater Expectations: A Shared Responsibility

Greater Expectations mean ...

A REINVIGORATED LIBERAL EDUCATION OF HIGH QUALITY FOR ALL STUDENTS. They also mean new student responsibility for learning, different emphases for faculty work, coherent institutional processes, outcomes aligned across educational levels, and a better public understanding of the value of college. How can the country achieve these important goals?

The answers involve collaboration and concerted action. Greater Expectations demand commitment from all groups and individuals interested in education; no one is exempt from participation. Raising the level of student accomplishment cannot be achieved simply by tweaking the college curriculum or extending the high school year. Higher education alone cannot solve the problems. Policies play a role by directing public attention and funds, but so do faculty and employer expectations. While isolated actions contribute to solutions, they are more effective when part of a comprehensive design for change. The New Academy described in this report offers such a design. It can be constructed from all the existing innovations in higher and secondary education, nourished by good will, and supported by collective, enlightened decisions.

College education in the New Academy is shaped by principles that build from and extend those of the recent past. They approach the teaching-learning collaboration with a consistent emphasis on learning, and they repeatedly reinforce the relevance of liberal education for a changing world.

Organizing Educational Principles: From the Present to the New Academy

Former or present...	modified...	present or future...
focuses on teaching	in recognition that what is taught is not always what is learned	ALSO focuses on learning
emphasizes what an educated person should know	in recognition of the explosion of available information	ALSO emphasizes where to find needed information, how to evaluate its accuracy, and what students can do with their knowledge
sees the curriculum predominantly as a conveyor of well-established knowledge	in recognition of the world's diverse complexity	ALSO interprets education as an informed probing of ideas and values
emphasizes study in a discipline	in recognition of the multi-disciplinary approach needed to understand real world problems	ALSO seeks connections within and across disciplines
emphasizes individual work	given the need to work as members of teams in the workplace and in community life	ALSO values collaborative work, particularly in diverse groups
stresses critical thinking	given the need for civic engagement in major policy decisions	ALSO links critical thinking to real-life problems, often involving contested values
promotes objective analysis	in recognition of the need to shape the rapid pace of change	ALSO develops creativity by valuing personal experience
studies majority Western cultures, perspectives, and issues	to respond to the plurality of the modern world, worldwide problems, and interdependence	ALSO learns about cultural complexity, a range of cultures, and global issues
values learning for learning's sake	to acknowledge the new role of higher education in U.S. society	ALSO celebrates practical knowledge
assumes a relatively homogeneous group of students	given the near-universality of college attendance	recognizes a diversity of students
considers higher education in isolation from primary and secondary education	given the need to build an aligned system to reach greater expectations	sees college learning as a part of a continuum with, and dependent on, the K-12 learning environment

Enterprise-wide problems require comprehensive solutions, even as the implementation details vary from one locale to another. At the collegiate level, student mobility within the educational landscape makes each institution, *de facto,* part of a larger national endeavor. Since learning is cumulative, both primary and secondary education contribute to college readiness. The universities themselves cycle back into the picture as the source of the next generation of school teachers, and as the site of graduate study by future professors.

Shared responsibility and collective action can occur at many levels— within institutions, across campuses, between K-12 and higher education, among stakeholders. All such collaboration will advance the country toward a true educational system, one that like ascending stairs leads all students toward higher achievement.

The following pages summarize the Greater Expectations New Academy, comprised of diverse institutions all moving forward together, although along distinct paths.

STORY

Comprehensive Change to Improve Undergraduate Learning

Some people fault higher education for a perceived resistance to change. While at times this may be true, these critics will be surprised by what they find on the many campuses, both large and small, where comprehensive change has significantly improved undergraduate learning. Examples exist all across the country—from CENTRAL CONNECTICUT STATE UNIVERSITY in New England, to the UNIVERSITY OF MICHIGAN in the heartland, to the UNIVERSITY OF SOUTHERN CALIFORNIA on the West Coast. Innovations in curricula, teaching methods, assessment, faculty support, and internal processes have coalesced into a true learning-centered environment. Not content with fine-tuning a course here or a requirement there, these campuses, and others like them, are re-envisioning their practices with a single goal in mind: to ensure better student learning for the twenty-first century.

The Greater Expectations New Academy includes ...

A RIGOROUS, PRACTICAL LIBERAL EDUCATION FOR

ALL STUDENTS BUILT ON . . .

- the belief that all students are capable of high level learning
- a commitment to inclusiveness and equal access to high quality college education for all individuals and groups
- clear and coherent expectations of achievement, aligned throughout educational levels
- solid preparation for challenging college work achieved through excellent K-12 teaching and curricula
- a focus on learning and the quality of student accomplishment
- a culture of intentionality at all educational levels: explicit goals achieved through appropriate practices and strategic allocation of resources
- a culture of evidence based on assessment and accountability
- public support for universal higher achievement
- joint responsibility and concerted action by all stakeholders.

ENACTED THROUGH . . .

An educational system that

- coordinates expectations for learning vertically through the years and horizontally across subjects and institutions
- progressively develops intellectual capacities, knowledge in essential areas, and ethical and civic responsibility
- serves a diversity of learning styles, life experiences, and enrollment patterns
- meets students at their ability levels and moves them all toward greater achievement
- clearly communicates goals and achievements to the public
- recognizes the need of society for skilled, knowledgeable graduates prepared for work, citizenship, and a rewarding life in the twenty-first century.

Colleges and universities that

- value themselves as learning communities whose mission is to improve student achievement
- respond to the students they serve: their diversity, enrollment patterns, preparation, aspirations
- assign resources to support increased faculty attention to student learning
- accept responsibility for improved teacher education
- promote collaborative leadership among the faculty, administrators, and other key stakeholders
- join with state and business leaders to align college with society's needs
- as a group, offer multiple educational models.

College and university faculty members who

- hold themselves to high standards of teaching
- hold their students to high standards of intellectual work that require strong commitments of time and attention
- set clear, interrelated goals for their courses, academic programs, and student learning
- accept responsibility for, and teach to achieve, the goals
- design coherent curricula and employ teaching practices to help all students achieve the goals
- regularly assess their own and student success, and use the results to improve learning
- individually and collectively assume responsibility for the entire curriculum
- embody life-long learning by engaging in professional development to improve teaching.

A curriculum that

- prepares all students for successful careers, enriched lives, and engaged U.S. and global citizenship
- develops self-directed, integrative, intentional learners who are empowered, informed, responsible, and thoughtfully reflective about their education
- is based on a practical liberal education in which students learn and apply their learning in multiple ways to complex problems
- is characterized by a diversity of perspectives
- is informed by technology and develops information literacy
- sets high standards of performance, but without prescribing a standardized path.

Classroom practices that

- while teaching knowledge, also ask students to apply it
- stress inquiry and engagement with unscripted and contested problems, including those drawn from real life
- in an intentional way, employ the diversity of the student body as a learning tool
- develop and value collaborative as well as individual achievement.

To achieve Greater Expectations, the National Panel strongly recommends ...

ENLIGHTENED PUBLIC POLICIES TIED TO CONCERTED ACTION. College learning has assumed a new centrality in our knowledge-intensive society. While the complexity and importance of the challenges presented by higher education's new role certainly warrant a long list of recommendations, the panel selected the most important and grouped them under five broad headings. They indicate commitments needed from society, as well as changes in education itself. The action steps highlighted throughout the narrative are repeated here as examples of specific initiatives through which change can occur.

Recommendations

IMPLEMENT POLICY IN SUPPORT OF GREATER ACHIEVEMENT:

All stakeholders commit to the dual policy goals of universal access to college learning of high quality and preparation for all students to succeed at this demanding level.

IMPORTANT ACTION STEPS

- Produce standards and assessments that focus on intellectual capacities and reflect the complex nature of learning and learning styles.
  INITIATORS OF ACTION: State and federal policymakers, informed by conversations with educational leaders.
- Base institutional accountability on demonstrated student success in achieving liberal education outcomes.
  INITIATORS OF ACTION: State and federal policymakers, boards of trustees, accrediting associations.
- Provide sustained resources for universal readiness and college success.
  INITIATORS OF ACTION: State and federal policymakers, school boards.

EXPECT GREATER ACHIEVEMENT:

Secondary and collegiate educators articulate and implement clear, aligned goals for learning to guide students purposefully from high school through college.

IMPORTANT ACTION STEPS

- Organize regular, continuous conversations between high school and college educators about learning outcomes, curricula, and teaching practices.

  INITIATORS OF ACTION: College professors and high school teachers.

- Expect high school seniors to complete a substantial, integrative piece of independent work to demonstrate their readiness for college-level work.

  INITIATORS OF ACTION: High school teachers and principals.

- Create a mechanism to coordinate advanced placement, dual enrollment, and remedial college courses.

  INITIATORS OF ACTION: Professors from community colleges, baccalaureate-granting colleges, and universities; high school teachers; and the organizations responsible for national assessments of educational quality.

- Expect college seniors to complete an integrative, capstone experience as evidence of advanced college-level learning.

  INITIATORS OF ACTION: College and university professors and employers.

REACH GREATER ACHIEVEMENT ON INDIVIDUAL CAMPUSES:
Colleges and universities commit to becoming intentional, learning-centered institutions and set timetables for achieving these goals.

IMPORTANT ACTION STEPS

- Each college and university sets explicit goals for student learning so academic department and general education outcomes can align with them.
  INITIATORS OF ACTION: College and university faculties.

- Colleges and universities implement curricula to develop student knowledge and intellectual capacities cumulatively and sequentially, drawing on all types of courses (general education, the major, electives) and non-course experiences.
  INITIATORS OF ACTION: College and university faculties and deans.

- Faculty members across disciplines and departments assume collective responsibility for the entire curriculum to ensure every student an enriching liberal education.
  INITIATORS OF ACTION: College and university faculties.

- College and university faculty members focus on important student outcomes, regularly assess student progress, base teaching on research about learning, and raise expectations of student achievement.
  INITIATORS OF ACTION: College and university faculties.

- Centers of teaching and learning on every campus make available significant resources to support faculty members as they assume the responsibilities of learning-centered education.
  INITIATORS OF ACTION: College and university deans.

- Faculty reward systems value learning-centered education.
  INITIATORS OF ACTION: College and university faculties and deans.

- Campus leaders place their institution's vision of liberal education at the center of strategic planning efforts and resource allocation.
  INITIATORS OF ACTION: Presidents, boards of trustees, chief academic officers, and deans.

PREPARE FOR GREATER ACHIEVEMENT THROUGHOUT THE
ENTIRE SYSTEM OF EDUCATION:

While students assume more responsibility for their studies, each
college, university, and high school commits to functioning as part of
a larger system to improve the level and quality of student learning.

IMPORTANT ACTION STEPS

- Restructure the professional preparation of elementary and secondary
  school teachers to give them deep knowledge of the disciplines
  they will teach, as well as of effective teaching strategies.
  INITIATORS OF ACTION: Faculties of arts and sciences and
  education, state boards of education, education program accrediting
  associations.
- Reform doctoral education so college professors are prepared to
  be effective educators as well as scholars.
  INITIATORS OF ACTION: University graduate faculties, in partnership with faculties in undergraduate colleges of every kind.
- Develop robust academic advising systems to explain the high
  expectations of college-level learning and help students map coherent pathways through a landscape of many institutions and programs.
  INITIATORS OF ACTION: College and university faculty members
  and advisors, secondary school teachers and advisors.

CREATE BETTER PUBLIC UNDERSTANDING OF THE
VALUE OF COLLEGE LEARNING:

All educators and other stakeholders consistently share with the public
the reasons why a practical liberal education is the best preparation for
all students in a rapidly changing world.

IMPORTANT ACTION STEPS

- Initiate, participate in, and sustain public dialogues about the goals
  of a contemporary liberal education and how they serve individuals
  and society.
  INITIATORS OF ACTION: College and university leaders, business
  leaders, national associations, students, and parents.
- Create and then implement a concept of rating and ranking colleges
  based on success in educating students that is flexible enough to
  suit a broad range of institutional missions.
  INITIATORS OF ACTION: College and university leaders, national
  media, and foundations.

Our call to action . . .

CARRIES A SENSE OF URGENCY. Monthly, economic and social structures suffer from conflicting priorities and questionable judgments; they seek guiding values and insight. Weekly, the workplace awaits more competent and adaptable employees. Daily, the world's problems cry out for reasoned responses. Everyone is responsible for meeting these needs, and no person can be relieved of his or her personal or collective obligation. Higher education must rise to the challenge by enabling all who attend college to become the empowered, knowledgeable, and principled citizens the interconnected globe requires.

The Greater Expectations National Panel, as a diverse group of individuals in conversation with colleagues around the country, examined the aims of college education for a knowledge-based society. The analysis in this report suggests that a New Academy, with learning at its center, is emerging as the answer to what college aspirants and society need for the future. Bringing this New Academy to its full potential—with the universal, high expectations it embodies—will depend on concerted and purposeful action arising from multiple strategic alliances. To fulfill its promise to today's students, those of future generations, and to the broader public, higher education itself will need to change; this report outlines the shape of the change.

Progression from the present situation to the New Academy will entail several conceptual shifts. First, colleges and universities must themselves assume a learning posture, improving their knowledge of effective education in the service of the common good. The exciting innovations described throughout this report and already flourishing on many campuses attest to the academy's potential to take on this role. Second, mutually sustaining partnerships—at all levels, with all stakeholders—involving enlightened policy decisions supported by concerted action need to become a regular feature of the educational landscape. These partnerships can be seen as the first step in creating a shared responsibility for success.

Finally, from these rich and intertwined alliances, we look forward to the growth of a true learning society, one that prizes creative intellectual activity as the basis for personal growth, practical intelligence, moral leadership, economic success, and societal strength. This is the final conceptual shift, to a culture that celebrates all manifestations of powerful and continuous learning.

Our pledge . . .

AS MEMBERS OF THE GREATER EXPECTATIONS NATIONAL PANEL, is to contribute to building both this New Academy and an inclusive learning society. To do so, we will serve as strong advocates and engaged leaders. We pledge further to accept the responsibility, in both our professional and personal communities, of giving life to the action steps and recommendations of our report. We invite all readers to do likewise and join with us to achieve the Greater Expectations new vision for learning as our nation goes to college. ■

ENDNOTES

1   Barbara Schneider and David Stevenson. 1999. *The Ambitious Generation*. New Haven and London: Yale University Press. p. 5.

2   *Chronicle of Higher Education Almanac Issue 2001-2002*, 48:1. p. 20. Also, National Center for Education Statistics. 2001. *Digest of Education Statistics, 2000*. Washington, DC: U.S. Government Printing Office. Chapter 3: Postsecondary Education. Table 175. *Digest* available at http://nces.ed.gov/pubs2001/digest/dt175.html.

3   The Education Trust. 1999. Ticket to nowhere. *Thinking K-16*, 3:2. p. 8.

4   The Education Trust-West. 2002. *The High School Diploma: Making It More Than an Empty Promise*. Prepared for Senate Standing Committee on Education hearing on Senate Bill 1731, April 2002.

5   Barbara Schneider and David Stevenson. 1999. *The Ambitious Generation*. New Haven and London: Yale University Press. p. 5.

6   National Center for Education Statistics. 2002. *Digest of Education Statistics, 2001*. Washington, DC: U.S. Government Printing Office. Chapter 3: Postsecondary Education. Available at http://nces.ed.gov/pubs2002/digest2001/ch3.asp#1. Also, Anthony P. Carnevale and Richard A. Fry. 2001. Economics, demography and the future of higher education policy. *Higher Expectations: Essays on the Future of Postsecondary Education*. Washington, DC: National Governors Association. p. 16.

7   National Center for Education Statistics. 2002. *Digest of Education Statistics, 2001*. Washington, DC: U.S. Government Printing Office. Chapter 3: Postsecondary Education. Table 247. Available at http://nces.ed.gov/pubs2002/digest2001/tables/dt247.asp.

8   The Education Trust. 1999. Ticket to nowhere. *Thinking K-16*, 3:2. p. 8.

9   National Center for Education Statistics. 2001. *The Condition of Education 2001*. Washington, DC: U.S. Government Printing Office. Table 29-3.

10   Clifford Adelman. 1998. The kiss of death? *National Crosstalk*, 6:3.

11   Clifford Adelman. 1991. *Answers in the Tool Box: Academic Integrity, Attendance Patterns, and Bachelor's Degree Attainment*. Washington, DC: U.S. Government Printing Office. Table 18.

12   *Chronicle of Higher Education Almanac Issue 2001-2002*, 48:1. p. 20. Calculated from other statistics provided.

13   National Center for Education Statistics. 2002. *The Condition of Education 2002*. Washington, DC: U.S. Government Printing Office. p. 25-40. Available at http://nces.ed.gov/pubsearch/pubsinfo.asp?pubid=2002025.

14   Anthony P. Carnevale and Richard A. Fry. 2001. Economics, demography and the future of higher education policy. *Higher Expectations: Essays on the Future of Postsecondary Education*. Washington, DC: National Governors Association.

15   National Center for Education Statistics. 2002. *Digest of Education Statistics, 2001*. Washington, DC: U.S. Government Printing Office. Chapter 3: Postsecondary Education. Available at http://nces.ed.gov/pubs2002/digest2001/ch3.asp#1.

16   Dana Markow, Sarah Fauth, and Diana Gravitch. 2001. *MetLife Survey of the American Teacher: Key Elements of Quality Schools*. New York: Metropolitan Life Insurance Company.

17   Adam Gamoran. 1992. The variable effects of high school tracking. *American Sociological Review*, 57. p. 812-828.

18   From a presentation by Robert P. Moses. 2/9/02. First meeting of Montgomery Co., (MD), Education Forum (MCEF), Washington, DC.

19   Karen M. Schilling and Karl Schilling. 1999. Increasing expectations for student effort. *About Campus*, 4:2.

20   National Center for Education Statistics. 2002. *Digest of Education Statistics, 2001*. Washington, DC: U.S. Government Printing Office. Chapter 3. Postsecondary Education. Table 172. Available at http://nces.ed.gov/pubs2002/digest2001/tables/dt172.asp.

21   Calculated from U.S. Census figures available at http://www.census.gov.

22   Data on community college growth available at http://www.aacc.nche.edu.

23   Total calculated from information in the Prentice-Hall Document Library, North Carolina State University. See http://www.hcl.chass.ncsu.edu/garson/dye/docs/gibill.htm.

24   National Center for Education Statistics. 2001. *Digest of Education Statistics, 2000*. Washington, DC: U.S. Government Printing Office. Chapter 4. Federal Programs for Education and Related Activities. See especially data in Table 359. Available at http://www.nces.ed.gov/pubs2001/digest/dt359.html.

25   Harold W. Stevenson and James W. Stigler. 1992. *The Learning Gap*. New York: Summit Books. Chapter 5.

26   Robert Rothman. 2000. *Bringing All Students to High Standards: Report on National Education Goals Panel Field Hearings*. Washington, DC: National Education Goals Panel. p. 4. Available at http://www.negp.gov/page9-3.htm#Std. Also, Jim Barlow. 1999. Bringing quality into the schools. *The Houston Chronicle*, Sunday, July 25,1999. Business Section. p. 1.

27   Anthony P. Carnevale. 2000. *Help Wanted . . . College Required.* Leadership 2000 Series. Princeton, NJ: Educational Testing Service. Figures 9, 26.

28 Thomas Ehrlich. 2000. Civic engagement. *Measuring Up 2000*. San Jose, CA and Washington, DC: National Center for Public Policy and Higher Education. p. 177.

29 Data cited in first three bullets from Anthony P. Carnevale. 2000. *Help Wanted . . . College Required*. Leadership 2000 Series. Princeton, NJ: Educational Testing Service. Figures 3, 26.

30 Tracey King and Ellyne Bannon. 2002. *At What Cost?* Washington, DC: The State PIRG's Higher Education Project. Available at http://www.pirg.org/highered/atwhatcost.html.

31 L. J. Sax, A. W. Astin, W. S. Korn, and K. M. Mahoney. 2000. *The American Freshman: National Norms for Fall 2000*. Los Angeles: Higher Education Research Institute, UCLA. p. 27.

32 Business Higher-Education Forum. 1999. *Spanning the Chasm: A Blueprint for Action*. Washington, DC: American Council on Education-National Alliance of Business.

33 Karen M. Schilling and Karl Schilling. 1999. Increasing expectations for student effort. *About Campus*, 4:2.

34 Data in first three bullets from John Immerwahr and Tony Foleno. 2000. *Great Expectations: How the Public and Parents—White, African American, and Hispanic—View Higher Education*. New York: Public Agenda.

35 Ford Foundation Campus Diversity Initiative Public Information Project. 1998. *National Survey of Voters*. New York: Ford Foundation. Summary available at http://www.diversityweb.org/Leadersguide/CCC/Community_response/nat_poll.html.

36 The 40 percent figure is for 4-year degree programs from Clifford Adelman. 1991. *Answers in the Tool Box: Academic Integrity, Attendance Patterns, and Bachelor's Degree Attainment*. Washington, DC: U.S. Government Printing Office. p. viii. The 60 percent figure is for community colleges and comes from ACT, Inc. See http://www.act.org/news/releases/2001/charts4.html. Because these are 3-year graduation rates for community college students, longer term completion rates may be somewhat higher.

37 National Commission on the High School Senior Year. 2001. *Raising Our Sights*. Princeton: Woodrow Wilson National Fellowship Foundation. p. 9. Available at http://www.commissiononthesenioryear.org/Report/report.html.

38 Available at http://www.ed.gov/pubs/NatAtRisk/title.html.

39 Several states are using tests that probe for more than factual recall including Maryland (Maryland School Performance Assessment Program), New York (Regents Examinations), and Vermont (the Comprehensive Assessment System that includes local portfolio assessments to complement statewide testing).

40 All quotations from personal conversation with Paul Schwarz, May 2002.

41 National Commission on the High School Senior Year. 2001. *The Lost Opportunity of Senior Year: Finding a Better Way*. p. 11-19. Available at http://www.commissiononthesenioryear.org/Report/report.html.

42   Association of American Colleges. 1985. *Integrity in the College Curriculum*. Washington, DC. p. 2.

43   However, in the most innovative colleges and universities, such as the sixteen identified through AAC&U's Greater Expectations Leadership Institutions national competition in 2000, more coherent curricula are appearing. Many of the seventy-three applicants to this competition demonstrated a beginning commitment to greater curricular coherence. See http://www.aacu.org/gex/Consortium/consortium.cfm for a list of innovative institutions.

44   Over the past decade, the Preparing Future Faculty Program, jointly sponsored by AAC&U and the Council of Graduate Schools, has engaged graduate departments across the country in revising doctoral education to include preparation for teaching and professional service. For a complete description, see Jerry Gaff, Anne S. Pruitt-Logan, Richard A. Weibl, *et al*. 2000. *Building the Faculty We Need: Colleges and Universities Working Together*. Washington, DC: Association of American Colleges and Universities.

45   Change may be starting to occur. In 2002, *U.S. News & World Report* asked colleges to supply information on many practices associated with greater student engagement.

46   Patricia Gurin. 1999. Expert report in "The compelling need for diversity in higher education," presented in Gratz, *et al*. v. Bollinger, *et al*., No. 97-75321 (E.D. Mich.). Washington, DC: Wilmer, Cutler, and Pickering.

47   Association of American Colleges and Universities. 1995. *The Drama of Diversity and Democracy: Higher Education and American Commitments*. Washington, DC. Also, Association of American Colleges and Universities. 1995. *American Pluralism and the College Curriculum: Higher Education in a Diverse Democracy*. Washington, DC.

48   National Center for Education Statistics. 1998. *The Condition of Education, 1998*. Washington, DC: U.S. Government Printing Office. Indicator 52. Available at http://nces.ed.gov/pubs98/condition98/c9852a01.html.

49   First three data items from Tracey King and Ellyne Bannon. 2002. *At What Cost?* Washington, DC: The State PIRG's Higher Education Project. Available at http://www.pirg.org/highered/atwhatcost.html. Last data item from Advisory Committee on Student Financial Assistance. 2002. *Empty Promises: The Myth of College Access in America*. Washington, DC. Available at http://www.ed.gov/offices/AC/ACSFA/whatnew.html.

50   The American Council on Education's series *On Change* provides useful insights into the process of institutional change in higher education. See http://www.acenet.edu/bookstore/index.cfm?alph=1.

51   David T. Kearns from the foreword to Denis P. Doyle. 2000. *Reclaiming the Legacy: In Defense of Liberal Education*. Washington, DC: The Council for Basic Education. Available at http://www.c-b-e.org/pubs/doylebk.htm.

52 Association of American Colleges and Universities. 1991. *The Challenge of Connecting Learning: Project on Liberal Learning, Study-in-Depth, and the Arts and Sciences Major*. Washington, DC.

53 Capstone experiences and other "high value" features of a curriculum foster student engagement with their education, an indicator of educational effectiveness. See George D. Kuh. Assessing what really matters to student learning: Inside the National Survey of Student Engagement. *Change*, 33:3. p. 10-17, 66.

54 *Reinventing Undergraduate Education: Three Years after the Boyer Report* (no author) provides details about student participation in research at the country's research universities and can be found at http://www.sunysb.edu/reinventioncenter/boyerfollowup.pdf. Such opportunities also exist at many other types of colleges and universities.

55 Orienteering principles derived from http://www.us.orienteering.org/Home.html and http://www.williams.edu:803/Biology/orienteering/.

56 "From 'My Work' to 'Our Work'." Title of American Association of Higher Education Conference on Faculty Roles & Rewards, January 19-22, 1995, Phoenix, Arizona, referring to R. Eugene Rice. 1994. Making a place for the new American scholar. *New Pathways Working Paper Series*. Washington, DC: American Association of Higher Education.

57 Clifford Adelman. 1991. *Answers in the Tool Box: Academic Integrity, Attendance Patterns, and Bachelor's Degree Attainment*. Washington, DC: U.S. Government Printing Office.

58 For more information see the PASS Web site at http://www.ous.edu/pass/.

59 For more information see the Standards for Success Web site at http://www.s4s.org.

60 Concept borrowed from Ralph Wolff, executive director, Western Association of Schools and Colleges, Accrediting Commission for Senior Colleges and Universities.

61 See the Greater Expectations Project on Accreditation and Assessment at http://www.aacu.org/paa/index.cfm.

GREATER EXPECTATIONS CONSORTIUM ON QUALITY EDUCATION

ALVERNO COLLEGE

BABSON COLLEGE

CENTRAL CONNECTICUT STATE UNIVERSITY

COLGATE UNIVERSITY

DUKE UNIVERSITY

EASTERN NEW MEXICO UNIVERSITY

THE EVERGREEN STATE COLLEGE

HAMPSHIRE COLLEGE

INDIANA UNIVERSITY-PURDUE UNIVERSITY, INDIANAPOLIS

KING'S COLLEGE

MOUNT ST. MARY'S COLLEGE (CA)

PORTLAND STATE UNIVERSITY

PRINCE GEORGE'S COMMUNITY COLLEGE

RENSSELAER POLYTECHNIC INSTITUTE

RICHLAND COLLEGE

STATE UNIVERSITY OF NEW YORK AT STONY BROOK

UNITED STATES AIR FORCE ACADEMY

UNIVERSITY OF HAWAI'I- KAPI'OLANI COMMUNITY COLLEGE

UNIVERSITY OF MICHIGAN

UNIVERSITY OF NEBRASKA-LINCOLN

UNIVERSITY OF SOUTHERN CALIFORNIA

WORCESTER POLYTECHNIC INSTITUTE